OUT
OF
ALL
TIME

Terry Boughner

OUT OF ALL TIME

with illustrations by

Michael Willhoite

Boston • Alyson Publications, Inc.

Published as a trade paperback original by
Alyson Publications
40 Plympton Street
Boston, Massachusetts 02118

Distributed in the U.K. by GMP Publishers,
PO Box 247, London, N15 6RW, England.

First U.S. edition: November, 1988

Library of Congress Cataloging-in-Publication Data

Boughner, Terry, 1940-
Out of all time.

Bibliography: p.
1. Gays — Biography. I. Title.
HQ75.2.B68   1988   306.7'66'0922   87-72882
ISBN 1-55583-104-4

Out of All Time
editor: Wayne Curtis
production and design: Wayne Curtis
proofreading: Tina Portillo
printing: McNaughton & Gunn Lithographers

Contents

UD WOMEN'S CENTER

To my beloved spouse,
Jerry Johnson,
whose love and faith
have led me to understand gay love
out of all time.

The Ancient World

The image of men loving men in the shadow of the Parthenon immediately springs to mind in any discussion of gay love in the ancient world. It is true that homosexuality was widely tolerated in Greece, but this was also true of many other ancient societies.

According to an Egyptian legend that dates back to around 3000 B.C., the god Seth said to the god Horus, "How beautiful are your buttocks! How flourishing!" Horus took this compliment to his mother Isis and, on her advice, refused Seth's proposition. Isis did not object to the idea of two gods having same-sex relations; she simply did not want her son to be the passive partner.

This story illustrates what was a common attitude toward homosexuality throughout much of the ancient world — an attitude that reappears throughout history. It was acceptable for a man to have sexual relations with another man as long as he was the active partner. Taking the passive role was shameful because it was seen as the woman's role.

The legend of Seth and Horus is only one of many gay stories that are found in the myths of ancient civilizations. *The*

Horus: Not a passive god.

Epic of Gilgamesh, for example, which is considered to be one of the great literary masterpieces of the Sumerian nation and which includes the first known account of the Flood outside of the biblical book of Genesis, has as its central theme the love story of two men.

The *Epic* is the story of Gilgamesh, a handsome Sumerian warrior who was told in a dream to expect the arrival of a mighty young man whom he would treat like a wife. When a young warrior named Enkidu arrived, he and Gilgamesh engaged in a fierce battle, which Enkidu won. Having proven his manhood, Enkidu developed a close friendship with Gilgamesh, and they experienced many adventures together. Enkidu was everything that Gilgamesh had hoped for. In fact, when Ishtar, the goddess of love, offered to marry Gilgamesh and present him with many gifts, he refused, preferring Enkidu to the goddess.

Unaccustomed to rejection, Ishtar sent an enormous bull to kill Gilgamesh. He and Enkidu killed the bull, and unwisely threw its testicles in the goddess's face. For that act, the gods condemned Enkidu to death and Gilgamesh to a life without his beloved companion.

After many years of grief and loneliness — and with his own death approaching — Gilgamesh begged the gods to allow Enkidu to appear to him and tell him what it was like to die. The gods agreed, and Enkidu appeared to Gilgamesh, telling him:

> That which you cherished
> That which you caressed
> is now devoured by worms...

Many ancient love stories end in grief, but the *Epic of Gilgamesh* accepted and praised the love of two men — as long as both of them conformed to the accepted definition of masculinity.

In ancient Babylon, where, as far as we know, no gay love stories existed, homosexuality was accepted in some periods, but only tolerated in others. While lesbianism was not mentioned, gay male love was defined by law. A man could not rape another man, nor have sex with a close blood relative. Further, he could not have sex with his neighbor's son. With these exceptions, homosexuality was permitted.

Homosexuality was also praised, even romanticized, in ancient China and Japan. During the Early Han Dynasty in China (206 B.C.-24 A.D.), men who preferred other men were called *lung-yang*, after a man of that name who was the lover of a fourth century B.C. prince. Another Han term for homosexual was *tuan-hsiu*, or "cut sleeve," from a story in which one of the Han emperors had cut off the sleeve of his garment rather than awaken his male lover, who was sleeping with his head on it.

The general attitude in these Eastern cultures was that, while homosexual sex was not as nourishing as sex between a man and woman, neither was it destructive. What was condemned, at least in China, was male bisexuality. The Han Chinese believed the children of a bisexual would be hermaphrodites.

Unlike Western cultures, Han China acknowledged the existence of lesbianism. The only concern that the Chinese had was that lesbians might wear themselves out by the excessive use of dildos. Like their Western counterparts, the Chinese doubted that women could experience sexual pleasure without a penis, or a penis substitute.

While Arabs and Asians were tolerant of same-sex love, and even considered it to be somewhat worthwhile, it was the Greeks who idealized it.

In the Hellenic culture, sex for the sake of sex alone was seen as a kind of madness, a sickness that had to be contained. To engage in sex simply because of lust, even if that lust was mutual, was considered dishonorable. True love was an irresistible force binding both body and soul. It was believed that one should always act with the good of the beloved as one's primary goal and always strive to keep the beloved's esteem. Lesbian love, however, never attained the same level of idealism in Greece as love between men. Although the first book of lesbian sexual practices was written by a Greek named Philaenis, lesbians — known as Tribads — were regarded as eccentrics.

As the Romans conquered the ancient world, they purposely imitated the art and manners of the Greeks, but they never truly adopted the spirit of Greek culture. Whereas the Greeks idealized same-sex love, the Romans only tolerated it.

The Stoic philosopher Seneca found same-sex relations distasteful. Cicero, on the other hand, wrote freely about the pleasure he derived from his slave-secretary's kisses. Of the poets, Catullus boasted of his male conquests, while Virgil liked only boys, and Horace repeatedly asserted that he liked both men and women.

Roman society set certain restrictions on homosexuality. It was illegal, for example, to rape a free-born citizen, and social custom condemned passivity. Slaves, however, remained outside of these laws and customs, and thus could play the passive role as their masters saw fit — even against their will. Of course, effeminate slaves were viewed with the same distaste as were effeminate free-born citizens. As in the Sumerian story of Gilgamesh and Enkidu, any man involved in same-sex relations had to conform to the accepted model of masculinity in order to be tolerated.

Nevertheless, homosexuals in Rome did have an accepted place in society. In the Colosseum and the Circus Maximus there was a section reserved for homosexuals. They came, usually on Thursdays and dressed in green, to root for their favorite gladiator or charioteer and commented loudly on what they considered to be his best attributes. The rest of the audience laughed and cheered them on.

The role of homosexuality in ancient societies varied from place to place and from age to age — but as many as five thousand years ago, homosexuals were an accepted part of these civilizations. There have always been men who loved men and women who loved women. Although this may never have been the orientation of the majority, men, at any rate, were able in these societies to express their homosexual desires without fear of repression. These pagan ancients understood human nature surprisingly well.

Akhenaten

They stood together on a balcony, looking out over the crowd below. One man was tall, perhaps in his late twenties or early thirties; the other was an adolescent. The older man was Akhenaten, the Pharaoh of Egypt's Eighteenth Dynasty. The younger man was Smenkhkara, whom the Pharaoh had just made co-regent. Smenkhkara may have been Akhenaten's brother, or a handsome servant who had caught the king's eye, but there is little doubt that he was in either case the king's lover. Akhenaten and Smenkhkara were the first documented homosexual couple in history.

It was the fourteenth century B.C. Moses had not yet been born, Athens didn't exist, and the site of Rome was still a swamp. In Egypt, however, the pyramids were already old. The Egypt that Akhenaten ruled had changed little for centuries. The clothing, language, religion, and government had remained more or less the same throughout the years.

When Akhenaten came to the throne in 1379 B.C., Egypt was the mightiest empire in the Middle East. The Pharaoh, who was considered divine, ruled over it absolutely. He was only one of the Egyptian pantheon of gods, however, and the greatest god was Amun-Ra. The priesthood of Amun-Ra was wealthy, numerous, and very powerful. No Pharaoh had dared to challenge their authority — until Akhenaten.

Akhenaten was born to be different. In a land where slender, well-formed bodies were admired, Akhenaten was almost grotesque. He had an elongated skull, fleshy lips, narrow shoulders, a pot belly, and enormous hips and thighs mounted on stork-like calves.

After his father's death, Akhenaten's ascent to the throne met with little enthusiasm. His wife Nefertiti was the more popular of the two; in sculptures and other artwork she appears twice as often as her husband. She bore four children, though it's doubtful any of them were fathered by the king.

In 1370 B.C., Akhenaten moved the capital of the empire from the city of Thebes to a new city called Akhetaten, translated "horizon of the Sun-disk." Akhenaten had begun a new religion — the first with only one god. He rejected the Egyptian belief in many gods, believing instead that there was only one omnipresent and omnipotent deity, and that this deity could not be represented in an earthly form. The only fitting symbol for this supreme god was the sun, and the only suitable offerings were prayers and flowers. Since the priests of Amun-Ra had their headquarters in Thebes, Akhenaten felt that his religion required a new capital. He therefore moved two hundred miles away from his rivals and set about the task of reorganizing Egyptian religion.

The clergy was horrified. In a society that hadn't changed in centuries, Akhenaten seemed to be acting like a desert whirlwind. He even changed Egyptian art, decreeing that the old, highly stylized images should be replaced by thoroughly realistic ones.

While the change in religion had important political results, Akhenaten was motivated by sincere religious faith. He neglected the empire in order to better worship his new god, wrote hymns to him — one of which may have inspired the

Akhenaten: No place for Nefertiti.

104th psalm — and in the process alienated the army, which had a vested interest in imperial advancement. Because he was so preoccupied with his new faith, the priesthood and the army were left without patronage or supervision, and they set up an alliance with the purpose of repairing the damage Akhenaten had caused.

It was at this point that Akhenaten fell in love with Smenkhkara, who strongly resembled Tutankhamen, better known as King Tut. An ancient painting, now in Berlin, shows Akhenaten and Smenkhkara naked, with the king gently stroking the chin of the young man, who is clearly deriving pleasure from the experience. In another relief, Smenkhkara is pouring wine for the king, and a third shows the two kissing.

Akhenaten expressed his devotion to Smenkhkara in as many ways as he could. He gave Smenkhkara the formal title "Beloved of Akhenaten," and to show that he had taken Nefertiti's place, the king also gave him the queen's reign name, "The Beautiful One is Come." Nefertiti was banished to a palace in the northern part of the city.

Meanwhile, the forces opposing the king continued to grow. Had Akhenaten and Smenkhkara returned to Thebes, acknowledged the power of the priests, and tended to the needs of the empire, the nature of their relationship would most likely have been ignored. Their idealism, however, blinded them to the approaching trouble.

The plan of the priesthood and the army was to kill the king and his lover and place Tutankhamen on the throne. Tut was young, and they thought he could be easily manipulated into restoring the status quo. Smenkhkara realized too late what was happening, and although he tried to prevent the rebellion, he was unsuccessful.

Tutankhamen was brought to Thebes to become Pharaoh, and every effort was made to blot out the memory of Akhenaten and Smenkhkara. Nevertheless, many carvings still remain in existence. The most touching reminder of this couple's love was Smenkhkara's coffin, unearthed in 1906. On its lid the following words were embossed:

> May I breathe the sweet breath that
> comes from thy mouth.
> May I see thy beauty daily.
> Mayest thou call my name for eternity.

David and Jonathan

One of ancient history's greatest love stories is found in the *Bible*. In a bold and moving Old Testament passage, Jonathan and David — one a prince, the other a future king of Israel — celebrate their love for each other.

The *Bible* gives a clear account of their love story in the book of I Samuel. David was the son of Jesse, a Bethlehem farmer of the tribe of Benjamin, the smallest of the twelve tribes of Israel. The small country was surrounded by enemies, the strongest of which were the Philistines. During one of the wars with the Philistines, David killed their champion Goliath, and was ushered into the tent of Israel's King Saul.

David was handsome, with a ruddy complexion and beautiful eyes. Jonathan, the king's son and heir, fell in love with David immediately. It proved to be a deep love.

From their first meeting, David went into battle wearing Jonathan's clothes and armor, winning victory after victory against Israel's enemies. His popularity grew — and with it Saul's jealousy. What made things worse was that Saul saw the love between Jonathan and David, and his rage increased until he began to plot David's death.

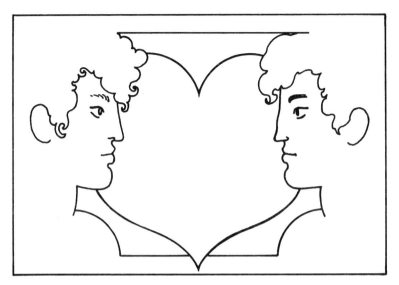

David and Jonathan: Passing the love of women.

Saul's plots were never successful. As he tried again and again to have David killed, Jonathan was always at David's side to help him escape from the king's schemes.

As the situation worsened, David stayed away from the royal court in fear for his life. One evening, when Saul wanted to know where David was, Jonathan lied to protect his love. The king became furious and said, "You son of a perverse, rebellious woman, do I not know that you have chosen the son of Jesse to your own shame, and to the shame of your mother's nakedness?" In the heat of his anger, Saul seized a spear and threw it at his son, barely missing his target. Jonathan stormed from the room. The next morning the two lovers met in a field, far from the king's eyes. They embraced and declared their love before God. "They kissed one another, and wept with one another."

The war against the Philistines continued, eventually claiming the lives of Saul and Jonathan. Upon hearing of the death of the man he loved, David grieved terribly and sought relief in writing. "I am distressed for you, my brother Jonathan," he wrote. "Your love to me was wonderful, passing the love of women."

Sappho

According to the ancient Greeks, the arts were inspired by goddesses known as the Muses, who descended the slopes of Mount Olympus, their feet clothed in mist. They sang in artists' ears and inspired them to create works of beauty. The writer Hesiod named nine Muses, but Plato added a tenth — her name was Sappho.

Strabo, the geographer and historian, wrote of Sappho that "in all of history you will find none to compare with her." Many since have agreed, including Ovid, Cicero, Lord Byron, and John Addington Symonds. Her verses were known everywhere in the ancient world, and her songs sung all along the shores of the Mediterranean.

Today, little remains of her work: the early church destroyed much of it for fear that its lesbian overtones would "infect" good Christians. Most of the approximately one-twentieth of her work that does survive is in fragments.

Sappho was born on the island of Lesbos sometime between 615 and 612 B.C. According to an ancient greek historian, she belonged to a prosperous family and had two brothers, Charaxus and Larichus, the latter of whom was ex-

Sappho: One of the Muses.

tremely handsome. Sappho, on the other hand, was described by two sources as small and dark, far from the Greek ideal of feminine beauty.

Sappho married and had a daughter, but little else is known of her marriage. Her husband supposedly died at a young age.

She lived in Mytilene, the capital of Lesbos, in a society that granted an equal place to women and men. This was rare in the ancient world, and it made it possible for Sappho to develop her creative gifts.

To support herself, Sappho began a school for young girls, taking them into her home and instructing them in dance, song, and poetry. She became deeply attached to some of the young women, and many of Sappho's finest poems were inspired by these same-sex loves. They were, she said, "hetaerae," or intimate companions.

Writing about Atthis, Sappho said that the girl caused a "delicate fire" to run through her flesh and brought on "a cold sweat." Her laughter "battered" Sappho's breasts and loosened her limbs. These lyrics clearly evoke Atthis's sensual, undulating walk, the soft curve of her buttocks, and the full roundness of her breasts. "I loved you," says Sappho to Atthis, "long ago when my own girlhood was still in flower and you were irresistible, bittersweet."

At some point, Atthis deserted Sappho for another woman's school. The poet mourned, "How beautiful was the life we led together. You used to perfume your body in my bosom." So great was this grief, she wrote, that she might as well have been dead.

Sappho outlived her grief, and other lovers followed. One ancient source tells of a girl named Gyrinna, who was to Sappho what Alcibiades was to Socrates. Another romantic interest was Gongyla, whom Sappho loved from the moment she laid eyes on her. After agonizing over whether she should love in silence, Sappho told Gongyla of her feelings, pleading,

"Hither to me tonight, I urge you, come Gongyla." Gongyla responded to the invitation, and their encounter "scorched" the poet.

As she grew older, Sappho's poems express a certain anguish. "Ah, girls, that I might escape my wrinkles." There is a plaintive sadness in her writing:

> The Moon has disappeared
> And the Pleiades have left the sky
> Midnight is near
> Time slowly passes
> And passes; yet
> Alone I lie.

Sappho was in her fifties when she died sometime around 565 B.C. By the time of her death, she had gained the reputation of being the finest living poet, and had loved many women. She would touch countless others in the centuries that followed through the beauty of the verse she left behind.

The Sacred Band

Every nation has its military shrines, cemeteries, and battle-fields where the valor of its soldiers is commemorated. In Greece there is a site which is unique: it commemorates the bravery of a unit manned entirely by homosexual men.

In 404 B.C., the thirty-year struggle between Athens and Sparta known as the Peloponnesian War finally ended. Athens, once the glory of Greece, lay in ruins. Her empire was gone and her fleet destroyed. The victorious Spartans ruled with a high-handed brutality that inspired the hatred of all the Greeks. This was particularly true in Thebes, a small city-state in central Greece where the Spartans maintained a garrison of their army.

According to the Roman writer, Plutarch, Thebes chafed under Spartan domination. Pelopides and Epaminondas, two young Theban men who were lovers, decided to resist the rule of the Spartans.

Pelopides came from a wealthy family, while Epaminondas was from a poor background. So that his wealth would not come between them, Pelopides lived in poverty with his lover. As they began to seek support among their friends for their

The Sacred Band: Beating the odds.

plan of revolt, the Spartans forced them to flee for their lives and seek sanctuary in Athens. They continued to gather support there, returning to Thebes in 378 B.C. with a small force of twenty-three pairs of lovers. They drove the small Spartan force out of the city and set up a committee to rule the state.

It was only a matter of time before the Spartans would return with a larger force. No city could match Sparta's wealth or manpower, but the Thebans formed an army that drew its strength from a different source: love. The Sacred Band was conceived as an army of pairs of lovers, men who would fight side-by-side with particular courage. It was made up of 150 pairs of men who had sworn their love to each other before all of Thebes in a ceremony at the tomb of Iolis, the lover of Herakles.

When the Spartans returned in 371 B.C. to try and reconquer Thebes, the Sacred Band was ready at the head of the main Theban army. They fought with a fury that astounded the Spartans and caught them unprepared. As the Spartans retreated, the Band pursued them, eventually killing the Spartan king and most of his soldiers. Theban independence had been won by the bravery of her gay men.

Twenty-two pairs of lovers had been killed, but these were quickly replaced by new members who had met the same qualifications. "Members of the Sacred Band," Pelopides was quoted as saying, "must not be addicted to the love or use of women but only to each other." And so it remained for nearly thirty years.

The Band, always fighting at the head of the Theban army, gave Thebes supremacy in Greece, almost capturing Sparta itself. One of the states Thebes conquered was Macedonia, and as a guarantee of good behavior, the Thebans demanded Macedonian hostages. One of these was fourteen-year-old Philip, future king of Macedonia and father of Alexander the Great. Philip came to know Epaminondas and Pelopides, and when he returned to Macedonia in 359 B.C. to become king, he resolved to imitate their success.

Philip had great plans for his country, and in 338 B.C. he led his army south toward Thebes. At the head of the force was the Companion Cavalry, a force built around Alexander and his lover Hephaestion and modeled on the Sacred Band. With twice the number of soldiers and better equipment, the Macedonians had the advantage. As the armies met on the Plain of Chaeronea, both forces knew their fate depended on the confrontation between the two groups of lovers.

In the end, Alexander's brilliance on the battlefield led the Macedonians to victory. The Sacred Band was pushed back and surrounded on a small hill where its members were slaughtered.

When King Philip arrived at the hill, he looked upon the carnage and wept openly. He ordered that the Sacred Band be given the full honors of war and buried where they had fallen — in the pairs as they had lived.

There is now a marble lion on that hill surrounded by a half-circle of cypress trees, a monument to the most valiant army that ever fought on a battlefield.

Alcibiades

Quickly, but with the practiced eye of the experienced host, the handsome young man surveyed the comfortable, richly appointed room. Everything seemed ready. The table was laid with fine silver, ready for the choice foods and vintage wines he hoped would please his guest. The couches on which they would recline while dining were covered with expensive cloth. The oil lamps gave a soft, warm glow, while through the garden window came gentle music from a slave's talented fingers. The mood was set.

Yes, he decided with a final approving look, all was ready. This time it *had* to work; this time the middle-aged man who would soon join him *must* make love to him.

Alcibiades had never before encountered a man who would not gladly return his favors. He was both handsome and wealthy, and he had a body which one writer called "sinuous, sensuous and seductive." Born around 450 B.C., Alcibiades was a golden boy in Athens' golden age. Even Zeus, it was said, would have deserted Ganymede just for a smile from Alcibiades.

But try as he might, he couldn't get the one man he desired to go to bed with him. That middle-aged man was the great philosopher Socrates.

Socrates was another famous figure in Athens, but the contrast between the two couldn't have been greater. Socrates, who waddled when he walked, had a large, awkward body and was not physically attractive. Yet the brilliance of his mind was almost legendary. He and his student Plato set many of our standards for thought, beauty, literature, and art. Alcibiades was the epitome of masculine beauty, and yet he, in his own words, "wandered around enslaved by this man as no one ever was by anyone."

They were together constantly, but many had to have wondered about the relationship. Alcibiades had been drawing attention to himself for years with his endless social engagements and his disregard of custom.

For example, the typical Athenian dress was a robe, or "himation," which customarily was white, and without decoration. Alcibiades wore himations of gold or purple with jeweled gold and silver ornaments or a crown of flowers in his blond hair. Once he attended the theater with a boyfriend, both of them wearing himations splashed with red to symbolize, he explained, the blood that flows between the hearts of two men in love.

But that blood was never too strong in any one instance, and one lover replaced another in quick succession. Until Socrates.

The great philosopher tried to teach Alcibiades that true love was of the soul rather than the body, but the young man didn't grasp the idea completely. Nor could he understand that Socrates wanted that part of him that had remained untouched — his mind. Sex could follow, but it would be unlike any sex the youth had ever experienced.

Socrates never understood Alcibiades' frustration. The young man loved him more than he had ever loved anyone. He

Alcibiades: Anyone but the man he wanted.

wanted to give the philosopher everything but had no idea how, since Socrates didn't seem to want or need what he had to offer.

Plato wrote that the turning point was the dinner where "nothing happened." The two men drifted apart, and Alcibiades went on to find military fame and glory. Nevertheless, his love for Socrates continued. At the age of thirty, just before gaining victory at the ninetieth Olympic Games, Alcibiades told Socrates, "It is to you that I owe everything that is good in me, if there be any."

Five years later there was a new man in Socrates' life: the young poet Agathon. One evening, at a dinner Agathon held for the philosopher, Alcibiades arrived uninvited and drunk. In a torrent of words that must have stunned the guests, Alcibiades told of the love he had for Socrates, a love that would not die after twenty years. Even now, he said, the sight of the older man made his heart leap into his mouth and tears come to his eyes.

Throughout this speech, Socrates sat silent and unmoved. Even when Alcibiades warned Agathon that the man he loved was both a "devil" and a "siren," and that unless he was careful Agathon would share Alcibiades' fate, Socrates said nothing. Only later did he comment, "I thought he would be better for my loving him."

By 399 B.C., Athens had tired of Socrates. He was brought to trial and convicted of the charge of corrupting Athenian youth. He was condemned to die, a sentence that was carried out by making him drink a cup of hemlock. To the end, he was surrounded by the young men who loved him. Alcibiades was not there.

The golden boy had also come upon hard times. After an increasingly checkered military career during which Alcibiades betrayed Athens, went over to Sparta, and betrayed the Spartans as well, he ended up in a city in what is now Turkey, living with an elderly female prostitute.

The Spartans successfully plotted to have Alcibiades

stabbed to death in 404 B.C. The prostitute dressed Alcibiades' corpse in her finest clothes for his burial.

In spite of his brilliance, Socrates hadn't mastered the human art of loving someone else. His verdict on Alcibiades — "I thought he would be better for my loving him" — reflects the folly of all lovers who try to change the nature of those they love.

Alexander the Great

In all of the ancient world, there are few figures who rival Alexander the Great in fame. At the height of his power he ruled most of the known world, and his life and legend are still a part of our culture nearly 2,400 years after his death. Less widely known is the fact that Alexander loved a beautiful man named Hephaestion and that their relationship gave Alexander the will to be great.

Alexander was born in July 356 B.C. His father was Philip II, king of Macedonia, a small state in northern Greece. His mother was Olympias, a beautiful woman with raven-black hair who claimed descent from the hero Achilles.

Hephaestion was born in 357 B.C. into the Macedonian nobility.

In appearance they complemented each other perfectly. Alexander had thick, curly auburn hair and fine features, the most striking of which were his large blue eyes. He was short and slender, even delicate. Hephaestion was taller than Alexander by a head and of a stronger build, with straight black hair, dark good looks, and walnut-brown eyes.

Alexander was King Philip's first son. Philip had lofty visions of Macedonia's place in the world and dreamt of leading his army against its traditional enemy, Persia. But to do that he had to win the support of the wealthier, more cultured Greek cities to the south.

These city-states wanted nothing to do with the plan of the Macedonians. To the proud Athenians, Thebans, Spartans, and others, the Macedonians were barbarians whose society was crude and whose pronunciation of Greek was barely comprehensible. The Macedonians had come late to Greek culture and learning, and the relationship between them and their southern cousins must have been similar to that between Americans and Europeans.

Philip determined that his son must have an education that no Greek could ridicule, and he summoned the philosopher Aristotle to come north and found a school. It was in this atmosphere that Alexander and Hephaestion met. According to an ancient source, the two students were inseparable from the beginning of their friendship. Aristotle was aware of their closeness and may even have encouraged it.

The king had no objection to the relationship either. In his past he had enjoyed relations with both women and young men. He was troubled when his son declared that his relationship with Hephaestion was permanent, since that meant Alexander would not provide an heir to the throne. Alexander could not be swayed, however. "Hephaestion is my soul," he is reported to have said. "I have no need of another."

The two ate together, studied together, and slept in the same room. The Greeks always assumed that in relationships like this sex played an integral part, but sex was actually only a small part of Alexander and Hephaestion's relationship. Alexander even went so far as to say that both sex and sleep reminded him of death. Accordingly, Hephaestion remarked that the most difficult battle he ever fought was "the battle of Alexander's thighs."

Even if sex wasn't paramount, their love was of the very

deepest kind. In their relationship, they were the most important thing in each other's life; it was a love in which the two became one spiritually. Their relationship was monogamous, committed, and permanent. After Philip was assassinated and the eighteen-year-old Alexander became king, even power couldn't come between them; Hephaestion never left Alexander's side.

Before Philip's murder, he had consolidated Macedonia's position as master of Greece and had begun preparations to fight Persia's Shah, Darius. Alexander continued the preparations, and in 334 B.C. he and Hephaestion led an army of thirty thousand into Asia.

They stopped at the city of Troy, where in front of their army they worshiped at the tomb of Achilles and Patroclus, the lovers immortalized in Homer's *Iliad.* They then marched on to crush the Persians at the Battle of Arbela. When Darius fled, he was in such a state of panic that he left his own mother to the mercy of the invading Macedonians.

When Alexander and Hephaestion went to meet the old woman, she was confused. Not knowing what Alexander looked like, she fell on her knees before Hephaestion, the taller of the two. One of her servants whispered her error to her, and she became afraid that she had offended Alexander. The king extended his hand and smiled, saying, "No, no good mother. For he too is Alexander." She joined their caravan and was a surrogate grandmother to them for the rest of their lives.

By 324 B.C., Alexander had in ten years created the greatest empire the world had known, stretching from the Aegean Sea to the Indus River. That summer, Alexander and Hephaestion were living in Hamadan, the summer residence of the Shahs. Hephaestion became ill with what is now believed to have been typhus. The best doctors labored over him, and his condition improved enough that Alexander considered it safe to leave his side for an important banquet. In the middle of the fes-

Alexander the Great: Battling his thighs.

tivities, however, a servant arrived with the news that Hephaestion's condition had worsened.

Alexander rushed to the palace where they had been staying. In the following days he kept his lover in his arms and allowed no one else to care for him. It was futile, however, and when those outside the room heard a cry so awful, so pitiful, that the gods must have wept at the sound, they knew that Hephaestion was dead.

Alexander's grief was as great as any man's nature could permit. For three days he stayed with the body of his lover and allowed no one to come near. He refused all food and drink and lay day and night with the corpse, as if he could somehow infuse life back into it. When he finally let Hephaestion's body be taken away for the funeral, an advisor remarked, "There is an empire, sire, and you are living." Alexander replied, "How can I live if one half of me is dead?"

Alexander ordered Hephaestion's funeral pyre to be the largest ever built, and throughout the empire all royal fires were to be extinguished, a symbolic gesture usually reserved for the death of the king himself.

With each day Alexander's sorrow deepened. He found refuge in wine, and his guards said that there were nights when they could hear him crying as if he would never stop.

On June 13, 323 B.C., Alexander was dying, and he called his generals to his bedside. His military leaders begged him to designate a successor, but he refused. With great effort he took the royal ring from his finger and let it drop to the floor. "To the best," he murmured. Alexander knew that the "best" was no longer among them. Not long afterwards, he and Hephaestion were together again.

Hadrian

It is a magnificent summer night in ancient Rome in the year 128 A.D. On Palatine Hill, home of the Caesars, soft breezes rustle the leaves of shade trees, while a pale moon bathes everything in its light. Two men, one fifty-two years old, one about eighteen, walk together on a quiet path. Without hearing their conversation, it's clear that they are the single most important human fact in each other's lives. They stop. Hands reach out in a shared impulse, fingers intertwine, and their lips meet in a gentle embrace.

While no such scene has survived in historical accounts, it certainly could have taken place. The older man was Hadrian, fourteenth emperor of Rome, who ruled from 117 to 138 A.D. The Roman Empire was at the height of its power, both militarily and economically, with boundaries stretching from Britain to Arabia. Over it all Hadrian presided, surrounded by power and money. For his age, he was in excellent physical condition. His body was lean and muscular, and his hair was thick, dark, and wavy. He had a ruggedly handsome face graced by grey-green eyes and a well-trimmed beard.

Hadrian: Antinous died that he might live.

But Hadrian was a haunted man. The writer Dio Cassius describes him as "reticent and withdrawn," a man filled with pain, searching, not for what he had lost, but for what he had never found. Perhaps this explains why Hadrian was the most widely traveled of Roman emperors. His predecessors had been content to stay in or around Rome, but Hadrian wandered throughout his empire, seldom able to stay in one place for long. Similarly, friends and male lovers came and went.

In 125 A.D., Hadrian returned to Rome, not knowing that his search would soon be over. At his palace he met a Greek pageboy named Antinous. Then about fifteen years old, Antinous had been born in Bithynia, a Roman province in what is now northern Turkey. He had thick, dark, curly hair, an aquiline nose, beautiful eyes, and sensuous, pouting lips which gave him a look of alert innocence. The Church Father Tertullian, who thought gay love was even worse than the love of women (both, in his opinion, were intrinsically evil), grudgingly admitted Antinous' beauty and asked, "Was Ganymede more fair?" Another contemporary said that Antinous "looked as if he had been created in a dream."

Although it is not clear how Hadrian and Antinous met, when they did there was an immediate joining of souls. St. Jerome wrote that their love was of "remarkable and memorable intensity." Another writer described it as "white-hot."

Although their age difference must have led to cynical comments about a "father-son" relationship or to insinuations that Antinous was only looking for a sugar daddy, all ancient accounts indicate that it was a true and solid love between equals. According to the writer Arrian, Antinous offered his lover "not only sex but love and sagacious, selfless counsel. His heart was wise. His intelligence, that of a grown man."

They also shared a curiosity about religion that Arrian called "a musing mysticism." In 128, the lovers left Rome to investigate Eastern beliefs. In Greece, they participated in an ancient rite celebrating death and resurrection which left them convinced that their love would survive the grave.

They traveled on to Syria, Jerusalem, and Egypt. In Egypt, like countless tourists before and since, they visited the pyramids and spent long days and nights cruising the Nile. But here, the priests and mystics they consulted foretold a coming tragedy: Hadrian would soon become sick and die.

While Hadrian was merely concerned, Antinous was extremely upset by the prophecy. Neither feared death, since they knew their love would survive it. But if one of them had to die, Antinous reasoned, it should not be the man on whom the Empire depended.

There was a widely held belief at that time that the voluntary death of one person, if done for love, could save or restore the life of the beloved. In the early morning of October 30, 130 A.D., Antinous went to the banks of the Nile, took a small boat, and set sail down the river. The frail craft was soon overpowered by the current, and the beautiful young man was killed.

Hadrian went nearly mad with grief. The body, recovered three days later, was embalmed and returned to Rome with the emperor, where it was buried in a secret place. It has never been found. Hadrian lived on in withdrawal and bleak despair for eight years, dying in 138.

Meanwhile, Antinous' sacrifice inspired people throughout the Roman Empire, and a new religion sprang up, adopting the idea that a sacrifice of love could regenerate the world. Hadrian's beloved became a divine symbol, or "paganism's last god." The fact that it was a homosexual love made no difference to the religion's followers.

The parallel of a love-inspired death that could save all mankind was uncomfortably close to Christian beliefs, and the early Church opposed the new faith. Hadrian and Antinous were condemned for their love, and this may have marked the beginning of the Church's hostility toward homosexuality. It took two hundred years, and finally the force of the Roman government, to end the worship of "the young sacrificial god from Bithynia." But the story of Hadrian's greatest love would not be forgotten, and it has inspired poets and artists ever since.

Elagabalus

The year was 222 A.D. Elagabalus, the eighteen-year-old emperor of Rome, stood at a window of his palace looking out over the capital. By day, the imperial city was a magnificent sight, but this evening all Elagabalus could see were hundreds of torches, carried by the rebellious citizenry.

The scene must have seemed unfair to the young king. Elagabalus had been born in the Roman province of Syria in 204 A.D. His grandmother and mother, both named Julia, were of royal blood, aunt and cousin respectively to the reigning emperor, Caracalla. The identity of Elagabalus' father was unknown.

Elagabalus was beautiful, with thick golden hair and a lithe bronzed body. This beauty became an asset when, as a duty of his royal heritage, young Elagabalus became a priest in the local religious cult. The primary symbol of this middle-eastern cult was a black conical stone that had fallen from the sky and was said to be the sun's penis. As a priest of the cult, Elagabalus would dance before the congregation of male worshipers, first clothed in radiant robes, then naked, as a tribute to the light of the sun.

After having excited the onlookers, Elagabalus would lead them to a high circular platform overlooking the stone. At his signal, the worshipers would masturbate to the point of orgasm, ejaculating onto the rock.

Elagabalus' grandmother had higher aspirations for the boy than the priesthood. Since the Emperor Caracalla had no heirs, she began circulating the rumor that Elagabalus was in fact his illegitimate son. The rumor spread rapidly among the local troops, who offered their support to the wealthy family.

Caracalla, meanwhile, was assassinated. After a brief challenge from another rival, Elagabalus was hailed as emperor and began the journey to Rome.

The beautiful young man did not know how poorly the people of Rome would view his "religious experience," or his effeminate mannerisms. Had he been older or wiser, he might have modified his behavior and given up the cult of the sun. But he had only his mother and grandmother to advise him, and their thoughts were elsewhere.

Elagabalus did not enjoy being emperor and escaped as often as he could to attend the chariot races in the Circus Maximus. About a year after ascending the throne, he spotted a Greek driver at the races who made his heart leap. The young driver was tall and well built, with curly black hair and brown eyes.

Emperor Elagabalus ordered that Hierocles be brought to the palace, bathed, and perfumed. Servants relayed the news to the impatient monarch that the young Greek was very well endowed. Hierocles would never race again; instead, he became the emperor's lover, companion, advisor, and eventually his spouse.

There was a public wedding ceremony, which no aristocrat dared miss. When the emperor appeared in the dress of a Roman bride, a murmur went through the crowd. After the ceremony, Elagabalus insisted that he be addressed as the wife of Hierocles. Later, when an unknowing guest addressed him in

Elagabalus: Treat him like a lady.

the usual manner with "Hail, Lord Emperor!" Elagabalus responded angrily, "Don't call me that, I'm a lady!" Within hours the story had spread throughout the city.

Certainly, Elagabalus was not the first gay emperor. But the Romans tolerated homosexuality only in men who conformed to accepted notions of masculinity. Effeminacy in a man, no matter what his station, embarrassed the society.

Although Rome sneered, Hierocles was good for his spouse. He encouraged the young emperor to become a better governor, gave him good advice, and kept away those who were trying to use the young man for their own profit. With the support of Hierocles, Elagabalus showed signs of becoming a competent ruler.

But the Romans either failed to recognize the change that was taking place or ignored it, talking instead of the emperor's latest gown or spreading the rumor that the emperor had asked a phyician for a vagina. As public indignation grew, Hierocles was warned that if he wanted to save himself he should leave. He refused to do so.

When the revolt began, it was led by the emperor's personal troops, the Praetorian Guard, who vowed their swords would draw the blood of the emperor and his lover before dawn. There are several versions of what happened that night.

One says that both Elagabalus and Hierocles were captured and killed and their bodies flung into the Tiber River. Unfortunately, this is the most likely scenario.

Another one is more poetic. According to this version, at the beginning of the trouble, Hierocles and Elagabalus put on peasants' clothes and slipped away from the palace. Under cover of the night they escaped into the countryside and eventually reached Athens.

In the centuries that followed, Elagabalus' name became a derogatory term applied to any public figure whose homosexuality became known, particularly those who, like the young emperor, fit the effeminate stereotype.

Jesus of Nazareth

Was Jesus homosexual? According to a number of Roman Catholic priests, the question of Christ's sexuality — and particularly his homosexuality — is frequently discussed among seminarians. The consensus, as one put it, "is often in the affirmative."

Making that definition on the basis of sexual activity is useless: there is no evidence that Jesus ever had a sexual experience of any kind. But given the traditional Christian position that Jesus was not just divinity in a human shell, but was divinity become human, then Jesus had to have felt the whole range of human emotion, including sexual attraction and love.

Who was Jesus attracted to, and who did he love? The four gospels portray a strong man of powerful character who was sensitive and compassionate. He was sometimes perplexed, angry, or scared, but he was also fond of parties, laughter, and good times with his friends. These sources record only three instances in which Jesus' love was directed at a specific individual: once in the Book of Mark and twice in the Book of John. In each case that individual was another man.

In Mark 10:17-21 there is an account of a man who asked about eternal life. "Jesus looked at him and loved him." This is the love of a teacher toward a prized pupil.

In John 12:35-36, Jesus is at the tomb of his friend Lazarus, who had died in his absence. It is here we have the only account of Jesus crying, or as John states, "Jesus wept." Those standing nearby commented on how much Jesus must have loved Lazarus. Jesus' sorrow over the death of his friend is evidence of a close bond, as is his role in the resurrection of Lazarus.

The third account, also found in John, is the story of the disciple who was referred to simply as "the beloved." The consensus of theologians, according to theologian Oscar Cullman in *The Johannine Circle*, is that the beloved disciple was the young John Mark.

Cullman writes that, from the context of the Gospel, John Mark was a man in his late teens. He was highly educated, had access to the highest priestly circles, and was at least moderately wealthy. He was not one of the twelve disciples, yet it is clear that Jesus loved him with a love that surpassed friendship.

According to the commentary in *The Anchor Bible*, on the night of the Last Supper, the couches around the table were arranged in the shape of an inverted U. Jesus would have been at the top. John 15:23 states that the beloved disciple shared that place with him. According to the original Greek, John Mark literally reclined on "Jesus' bosom."

The description is important and not used accidentally. Only one other time in John's Gospel does the author use those words — when describing Jesus' relationship with God as being in the "bosom of the Father." Thus, as Jesus is in the heart of God, so was John Mark in the heart of Jesus.

That evening was not a pleasant one. Jesus was going to die, knew it, and was frightened. Crucifixion was probably the most painful form of execution ever conceived. The situation was made worse by the fact that someone in the room — one of his students — would betray him with a kiss and set the chain of events in motion. Jesus shared this knowledge with those assembled.

Peter, traditionally the leader of the group, was not at the head of the table and didn't hear clearly what Jesus had said. He asked John Mark to have Jesus tell them who the traitor was. Raising himself up on one elbow to talk to Peter, John Mark then "falls back" to ask Jesus, "Who is it?"

Jesus whispered his answer and then said loudly to Judas, "Be quick with what you have to do."

The long night that would change the course of Western civilization wound to its conclusion the following day with Jesus naked and nailed to a cross. Jesus saw his mother and his beloved, and in words that must have been an agony to say, gave each to the other's care.

In the days following the Resurrection, Peter, Thomas, James, Nathaniel, John and "two others" went north from Jerusalem to Galilee. One of the others was John Mark. Beside the Sea of Galilee, Jesus appeared to them, fixed them breakfast and asked Peter three times, "Do you love me?" Three times Peter affirmed that he did, after which Jesus said, "Follow me."

Irritated that he was the only one questioned in this manner, Peter turned to John Mark and asked, "What about him?"

Jesus answered, "If I choose that he should survive until I come back, what does it matter to you?" The tone in the Greek is, "That's none of your concern."

Was Peter's irritation a symptom of jealousy over the special place that John Mark held in Jesus' heart — a place that Peter, despite his devotion to the Master, could not occupy?

John Boswell, in his book *Christianity, Social Tolerance and Homosexuality,* points out that "ancient societies recognized fewer boundaries between friendship and romance." In an intense relationship, such as the one John Mark and Jesus shared, Boswell says the erotic element "was assumed."

Jesus: Often in the affirmative.

In this light, the Christian Church's later hostility to homosexuality is much harder to comprehend. But no matter what the theological cover, what is important is that Jesus held a deep love for another man. That man was his close companion and confidant, and Jesus was not uncomfortable about expressing that love publicly.

These are lessons that most Christians have chosen to ignore.

Early Christianity

Slowly and insidiously it spread across Europe. For centuries it appeared to be a disease of epidemic proportions, and nothing could be done to stop it.

In 541 A.D. the Eastern Roman Emperor, Justinian, claimed that it had caused the deaths of one-third of the population of Constantinople. Two hundred years later, Charlemagne said that it was tearing his kingdom apart. Three hundred years after that, Peter Damian wrote in a letter to the pope that the disease was "a cancer eating at the heart of Christendom" that would lead to everyone's death if it wasn't stopped.

Certainly the Black Death that periodically ravaged Europe was terrible — people died by the tens of thousands. But Justinian, Charlemagne, and Peter Damian were not talking about the plague. They were upset about homosexuality. To them, homosexuality was not just a disease, it was the worst of all crimes. Damian even believed that having sex with animals was more tolerable than men having sex with other men.

There are many sources for Western homophobia. Many blame St. Paul, and others the Roman Stoics. The Stoics believed that life was best lived by keeping both pain and pleasure to a minimum. Too much of either one was dangerous because they distracted the mind from contemplating higher things. Sex, since it was necessary to continue the species, was tolerated, but only the procreative, heterosexual kind.

Christianity adopted many of the ideas of the Stoics, equating physical pleasure with sin, so that only the goal of producing children could make sex acceptable. Obviously, homosexual sex was considered morally reprehensible, since it seemed to have only pleasure to recommend it. St. John Chrysostom said it was the enormity of all vices. St. Augustine, although he had enjoyed a homosexual experience in his youth, also condemned it.

But this condemnation of homosexual sex was also partly a function of the Church's attitude toward women. As Chrysostom wrote, "By their nature, women are in a lower category than men." Much of the religious horror over homosexuality lay in the idea that homosexual men were acting like women, being penetrated, "defiling" the male body. Lesbianism was rarely mentioned; what women did was of no importance.

When Christianity became the state religion of Rome in the fourth century, this homophobic hysteria became law. Homosexuality became a crime in 342, and in 390 Emperor Theodosius set the punishment as death by burning.

In the sixth century, Emperor Justinian reorganized Roman law and codified it, forming the basis for many modern European legal systems. In the Justinian Code, homosexuals suffered castration and death.

Obviously, moral diatribes, decrees, and punishments couldn't eradicate homosexuality. Consequently, the Church redoubled its efforts. In 693, the Council of Toledo declared that "sodomists" had infiltrated the Church itself, and ordered that clerics who lay with men should be degraded, exiled, and damned.

Judging by the great body of penitential literature dealing with the subject, it seems that the Church fathers met with little success in their attempts to discourage homosexual behavior.

St. Augustine: He liked it too much.

The prescribed acts of penance for it are interesting. For example, a youth under twenty was required to make six fasts simply for kissing another man. Licentious kissing required eight fasts, but if it led to orgasm, the punishment was increased to ten fasts. For those beyond the age of twenty, the punishment for any of the above was bread and water for life and exclusion from church services.

By the early Middle Ages, a new argument was emerging against homosexuality: it was a sin against nature. According to this idea, everything had been designed for a purpose. Thus, the penis had been designed only to enter the vagina for the function of procreation. Anything else was unnatural.

As with many theological questions, St. Thomas Aquinas (1225-1274) consolidated the Church's thinking on homosexuality for centuries to come. Prefacing his remarks with the observation that all sexual activity likened man to a beast, he held that homosexuality was especially wrong because it was irrational, unnatural, proceeded from lust, and was only for pleasure. He *did* allow that two men could touch, caress, even kiss — if the motive was right. However, there was a danger that such contact could become *enjoyable*, and it was therefore safer to avoid it altogether. By the time of Aquinas's death, homosexuals had been defined as a separate group, condemned by the men who spoke for God and nature, and made outlaws throughout Europe.

The sodomy trials of sixteenth-century Geneva led to the execution of seventy-five men and boys between the ages of twelve and fifty. And the link in the popular mind between homosexuality and witchcraft made it likely that many more gay men died in the periodic witch hunts. Finally, the Church's Inquisition reserved the lowest cells in the deepest dungeons for homosexuals, most of whom didn't survive.

All the furor was over sex. The most powerful minds in Europe, for long centuries, seemed unable to grasp the idea that two men or two women might actually *love* one another.

The Papacy

While the Church was busy hunting down homosexuals among the faithful, then burning, mutilating, or otherwise killing them, there were often high religious officials finding "unnatural" places for their own private parts. There have been at least five documented homosexual popes. The actual number is undoubtedly greater, but church historians claim that there have been only five and that the last one died in 1555.

The earliest gay pope on record was John XII, who reigned from 955 to 964. His given name was Octavian, but when elected pope he changed his name to John, thereby establishing the custom of reign names which has continued ever since. John loved both boys and muscular young men. He rewarded those who were willing to sleep with him by giving them the most profitable bishoprics.

John was seventeen when he became pope and died when he was twenty-six — he had a stroke while having sex with one of his beautiful young men.

Benedict IX, who reigned from 1032 to 1044, was the next openly gay pope. One historian referred to him as the Christian incarnation of Elagabalus. Beyond that, we know little about him, except that he tried to resign from his office in favor of his Jewish godfather.

Over four hundred years passed before the next gay pope. In 1464, Paul II was elected to the office. He is supposed to have been the most handsome pope ever to reign. Like John XII, Paul died while having sex, but the cause of his death was strangulation.

After Paul II's death, the College of Cardinals convened quickly, and chose Francisco della Rovere, who reigned from 1471 to 1484 as Sixtus IV. Sixtus was from a poor family in the Italian city of Savona, but became the head of the Franciscan order. His nephew and lover, Pietro Riario, understood that money could work miracles, especially in the College of Cardinals. He bought the papal office for Sixtus, who richly rewarded the young man later.

Until his death at the age of twenty-eight in 1474, Riario ran the Church, approving of the Spanish Inquisition and plotting the murder of Lorenzo de Medici. He also made Rome a center for the arts.

After Riario's death, the stories about Sixtus' reign become more bizarre. In one account, he chose two of the most handsome, muscular young men he could find, had them remove their clothes, armed them with daggers, and watched them fight to the death. The survivor was his bed partner that night. Furthermore, Sixtus only chose adolescent boys and young men in their twenties for the College of Cardinals. Before the illness that led to his death, Sixtus was considering legalizing sodomy during the warm season, in response to the urging of his Cardinals.

When Sixtus was ill, the finest doctors in Rome were consulted, and they prescribed mother's milk. The pope suggested that the juice of young men would suit him better.

While it is likely that Leo X, who reigned from 1513 to 1521, was bisexual, the most openly homosexual of the popes was Julius III, whose reign began in 1550 and ended in 1555.

Julius III: Sex in St. Peter's.

Julius was sixty-three when he was elected pope after a long and contentious conclave. The future pope supposedly told the gathering that if he was elected he would make his seventeen-year-old lover a member of the College. He not only kept his word, but he gave the young man the post of Secretary of State, which was usually reserved for the highest ranking member of the group.

During his reign, Julius often summoned four or five of his teenaged cardinals for orgies in locations where other church officials would be sure to discover them. Many were horrified. Others, like the Archbishop of Benevento, were not — he wrote a book entitled *In Praise of Sodomy* and dedicated it to the pope. Julius was delighted by the compliment.

The Arab World

Beginning in the seventh and eighth centuries, the Arabs built an empire that stretched from the Arabian peninsula across North Africa and into Spain. With an almost fanatical dedication to beauty, they developed a civilization that combined delicacy and durability.

Unlike the Christian West, the Arabs didn't ascribe any particular superiority to either homosexual or heterosexual love. They felt that both were valid responses, but like the Romans disdained the passive partner. At the height of Arab civilization there was an outpouring of homoerotic love poetry, and homoerotic images can be found in much of Arab literature.

Much of this was due to the influence of the writings of the ancient Greeks which had been translated into Arabic. From Plato and Aristotle, the Arabs developed the idea of different types of love: the ordinary, "mahabbah," and the extraordinary bonding of two souls, "ishq." When two people experienced ishq it was believed they were in fact two halves of the same soul that had become separated in a past world. Along with death in a "jihad," or holy war, death for ishq assured direct acceptance into Paradise.

The Arab World: Two halves of the same soul.

Thus, suicide in response to the death of a lover was entirely justified, and even expected. Arab literature abounds with beautiful stories of men whose lovers followed them in death, only to have their souls reunited in Paradise for eternity. Only a poet could justify living on after his lover's death, because his pain would lead to the creation of beauty. One story told of a poet who lost his love, and delayed following him in death to write a poem in commemoration of their relationship. To console himself while he wrote, he drank from a cup made from a mixture of clay and his lover's ashes.

Writing of their love for other men, Arabs rhapsodized over jet-black hair lying softly against a white cotton pillow; of eyes like "dew drops from the rose"; of faces like "gardens of jasmine," whose sweet scent could drive other men "mad with desire." They sang of teeth like bubbles or "whitest snow on far-flung mountain tops," and of skin the color of silken gold or "soft brown with tinges of smoky rose."

Arab homosexual poetry stands today as the earliest known example of medieval romance lyric poetry.

William Rufus

William Rufus (1056-1100) was the son of William the Conqueror, the man who in 1066 invaded England and set himself up as king. William Rufus, according to the contemporary chronicler William of Malmsbury, was fairly good looking, being "thick-set with a muscular body, blond hair and sparkling eyes that seemed to change color in the light." Anselm, who was then Archbishop of Canterbury, said that the younger William was "courteous, jovial and bountiful."

Anselm would later change his opinion of William Rufus. When he became king in 1087, William Rufus, or William II, rarely shared his royal bounty with the Church. Furthermore, William II was homosexual.

William surrounded himself with some of the most beautiful men of England and France. According to the historian and monk Ordericus Vitalis, these beautiful youths went about in fancy dress, in "shameful contrast" to the court of William I, where spartan dress had been the rule. Even worse, these men, and even the king himself, wore their hair long when it was "well known that a proper Christian style demanded that men's hair be cut short."

William Rufus: Lights out in the palace.

All this was bad enough, but Ordericus goes on to declare that these men were sodomizing one another. The hair and the clothes indicated they were "given to effeminacy," and at night all the lights were out in the castle — a sure sign that something unseemly was going on.

William of Malmsbury agreed. "The court of the king," he wrote, "is a brothel of catamites." Men were going about holding one another's hands, and kissed one another in public so often that "it scarcely makes anyone blush."

No one was more open about his sexual preference than the king himself, who publicly declared his love for Robert Fitzhaimo, his constant companion. Ordericus sniped that Robert, ten years the king's junior, was "attending the king day and night."

When pious brothers of the Church complained about the king's sexual behavior, William replied that he would close all convents within three miles of a monastery if the noisy monks wouldn't be quiet. For that, William was accused of blasphemy.

Secular leaders were concerned over the king's behavior, but for a reason different from that of the Church: they worried that the king would not produce an heir. The dynasty was not very old, and without a clear successor, civil war could easily follow William's death. Still, William refused to consider marrying. Ordericus reports that some people suspected that William was impotent, but that Robert Fitzhaimo laughed in derision at the idea when it was presented to him.

Throughout his reign, William II put up with pressure from the Church and his lords, but continued to be devoted to Robert Fitzhaimo. In fact, his devotion probably cost him his life. On August 2, 1100, the king and his party went stag hunting. William became separated from the rest and was killed by an arrow wound in his chest. No explanation for the king's death was ever given.

Ordericus reports that the Church gave thanks to God and expressed hope that all sodomites might benefit from the lesson.

Edward II

One of the most well-known gay monarchs was Edward II of England (1284-1327), although his fame results largely from his gruesome death. Edward's story is very much a love story, and his devotion to his lovers led to his destruction.

Edward was tall and handsome, with red hair, fine features, and a muscular body. His first love was Piers Gaveston, a Frenchman whose dark looks complemented Edward's fair complexion. Piers was sensitive, gentle, and had a great sense of fun.

They met when Edward, then Prince of Wales, was fourteen and Piers was sixteen. The young Frenchman was brought to England by Edward's father to serve as a companion for Edward and to train him in weaponry. Instead, they fell in love.

Neither of the young men showed much prudence. They were extravagant and made no efforts to be discreet about their relationship. They made fun of the realm's great lords and barons, many of whom were as powerful as the king himself.

Edward's father sent Piers back to Gascony and arranged for his wayward son to be married to Princess Isabelle of France. But before the marriage took place, the king died, and Edward II became king in 1307.

Edward II: The cruelty of his death is legendary.

Edward's first act was to bring Piers back to England, although he did marry Isabelle for reasons of diplomacy. The princess was only thirteen, and so was no immediate threat to Edward's relationship with Piers. Shortly after the wedding, Piers was seen wearing Isabelle's jewelry, and he carried Edward's crown at the coronation.

Edward ignored his new bride, causing her to complain to her father that she was "the most wretched of wives. The king is an entire stranger to my bed."

The French king took action, supplying the English barons with funds for a rebellion. In 1311, Edward was forced to exile Piers, who went to Ireland to serve as the king's representative.

Although Piers was gone, the king still refused to have anything to do with his wife, and Piers returned to England a year later. When the barons again objected, Edward agreed to the formation of a committee to administer the kingdom — a group of twenty-one nobles to be known as the Lords Ordainers.

This idea might have worked, if it had not been for Queen Isabelle. She now nursed a great hatred for her husband and had some popular support in England. She also took the barons' leader, Thomas, Earl of Lancaster, as her lover.

The influence of Isabelle and her lover led the nation into civil war, and Edward and Piers fled London. As they were making plans to leave the country, Piers was captured and beheaded by the earl of Lancaster in June 1312. Edward collapsed in grief and rage. He took Piers' body, and buried it at the place where they first met.

With his lover gone, Edward returned to the throne, but did not rule. For a while he had relations with Isabelle, and they had a son, the future Edward III. The queen, however, could not compete even with Piers' memory, and she knew it.

After Edward's defeat, the barons named Hugh le Despencer, son of one of their leaders, as Court Chamberlain to watch the king. Hugh was tall and dark, resembling Piers in many ways. While he watched the king, Hugh fell in love with him. Hugh's attention helped Edward overcome his grief over Piers' death, and soon the two were involved in a relationship.

When the barons learned of this, the positions of both Hugh and his father were threatened, and they asked the king for his assistance. Again Edward and the barons went to war, but this time the king won, and he avenged the murder of Piers Gaveston by beheading the earl of Lancaster in 1322.

With the king now back in control, the queen felt compelled to take stronger action. With Roger de Mortimer, the barons' new leader and her new lover, she went to France to arrange support from her family. They returned on September 24, 1326 at the head of an army. With considerable popular support, their campaign was successful, and on November 16 they captured the king and his lover.

By the queen's order, the young Hugh le Despencer was publicly executed. He was stripped and tied to a tall ladder. The executioner first cut off his genitals and then cut out his bowels. Finally, he was thrown into a raging fire. The queen observed the entire spectacle.

Edward, no longer king, was moved from castle to castle, finally ending up at Berkeley, home of Roger de Mortimer. His clothing was of coarse wool, and his cell was over the charnel house. His jailers tormented him freely.

One night three men arrived in Edward's cell to end his life. He was stripped and tied to a heavy wooden table. His legs were drawn back until his thighs touched his chest and belly, and a red-hot poker was thrust into his rectum. He died during this parody of homosexual sex, and his screams could be heard beyond the castle walls in the town below.

Suleiman the Magnificent

During the sixteenth century, the nations of Europe were constantly at war over religion and territory. They also were threatened from the east by the Ottoman Empire, which ruled most of the Middle East, North Africa, and was gaining territory in Eastern Europe. From 1520 to 1566, the ruler of this grand empire was Suleiman, one of the most powerful men in the world.

Suleiman was born around 1495. He was quiet and sensitive, and loved poetry and music. Those who knew him called him a visionary and an idealist. He had a long thin body which he carried gracefully, a delicate complexion, and long thin hands.

In his adolescence, Suleiman's father gave him a Greek slave named Ibrahim as a companion. Ibrahim was two years older than Suleiman, and was tall, with dark, curly hair and a solid muscular body.

The two young men shared many interests, often discussing religion and philosophy. Ibrahim would play the guitar and sing, and the two wondered whether music and ideas might not be more permanent than Constantinople, the Ottoman capital.

Suleiman the Magnificent: Even love can be corrupted.

Ibrahim never left the prince's side, and it was common knowledge that Ibrahim shared the prince's bed.

When Suleiman became the tenth sultan of the house of Osman, he made Ibrahim his Grand Vizir, or head of the Imperial Council. Later Ibrahim was also named head of the army, making him second in power only to Suleiman himself. Since Suleiman trusted Ibrahim and had no real desire to rule, Ibrahim in effect became the ruler of the empire.

Neither of the two lovers realized the danger that these changed circumstances presented for their relationship. Ibrahim grew to enjoy his position and wealth, living in luxury and becoming even wealthier by accepting foreign bribes.

The qualities that he had originally admired in Suleiman began to seem absurd to Ibrahim. He began to feel that the sultan was a dreamer who would accomplish nothing and laughed at some of Suleiman's most cherished ideas.

Eventually, Suleiman became bitter and realized that the love he had shared with Ibrahim was gone. In 1534, the sultan heard a rumor that his Grand Vizir was plotting with an enemy to take over the empire.

Suleiman summoned Ibrahim for dinner. After eating, the two went together to the sultan's bedroom. The next morning, slaves found the walls streaked with blood and Ibrahim's naked body, which had been strangled with a bowstring, lying face down on the bed. Suleiman refused to allow the walls to be cleaned, and the stains remained until his death.

Although Suleiman went on to love again, the young Ibrahim was always in his heart. When one of the monarch's female partners mentioned Ibrahim and asked about their relationship, Suleiman replied, "I loved him above all others — even you."

American Indians

Christopher Columbus' physician on his second voyage to the
New World in 1494 wrote that it was "Detestable! Nauseating!
Disgusting!" In 1513, the adventurer Balboa, while exploring
what is now Panama, described what he saw as "abominable."
Most early observers of the native cultures of the Western
Hemisphere noted the prevalence of homosexual practices,
which only confirmed their view of these people as primitive
heathens who needed to be conquered.

One cynical theologian, Francisco de Victoria, countered
with the argument that if homosexual practices justified conquest, France was indeed holy by trying to conquer the Italians.
His statements were ignored.

Although there were homosexual elements in native cultures, the European horror stories were a mixture of truth and
fantasy. Among the Carib Indians on the island of Hispaniola
— whose behavior had inspired the disgust of Columbus' physician — there was widespread acceptance of a certain kind of
homosexual act. It was customary for warriors to castrate boys
that were captured from enemy villages and keep them as lovers
until they were about eighteen; they were then killed and eaten.

In 1526, a Spanish historian wrote that some Carib men also had lovers that they did not intend to smother in butter and spices. These lovers were distinguished by wearing "naguas," or short skirts. They also wore jewelry that their lovers had given them.

While the Caribs were a relatively poor and unsophisticated people, the Mayans, who occupied the Yucatan Peninsula of Mexico, were a wealthy and advanced civilization. Although their culture was declining when the Spanish arrived, there are accounts that they had accepted and even institutionalized homosexual relationships.

When a Mayan boy reached puberty, his parents asked him whether he wished to have a boy or girl for a companion and sexual partner. Most boys were expected to choose another boy, because it was thought that boys preferred each other. At about the age of eighteen, upon entering manhood, the young man again could choose between the two. If the youth chose a man, the relationship had to be permanent and monogamous. If he chose a woman, the relationship had to be permanent, but not necessarily monogamous.

Despite what the Spanish *conquistadores* wrote, not all Indian cultures accepted gay relationships. The Aztecs of central Mexico, for instance, required the death penalty for both male and female homosexuality. The methods for execution were brutal and were enforced. The Incas, in South America, burned men suspected of homosexual activity. Shortly after they were conquered by the Spanish in 1530, one observer wrote that in a town in northern Peru there were fifteen women for every man when the Incas finished burning the homosexuals. By 1580, when another visitor wrote, the area was still known for its gay activity.

After conquering the Indians, the Spanish set about the task of converting them, with an amusing result. A pious priest, Father Jose del Valle y Araujo, composed a novena to St. Boniface to help those trying to overcome their homosexuality. In-

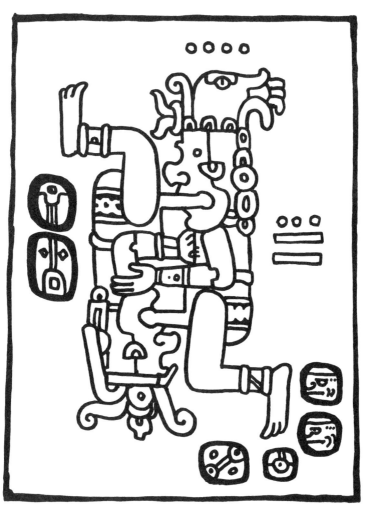

American Indians: A variety of approaches.

stead of praying to the saint for a cure, many gay Indians prayed to him for help against heterosexuals, making Boniface the "Patron of Homosexuals." The novena was popular for centuries; in fact, there is a woodprint dated 1821 with the caption "Patron of Homosexuals" which shows a handsome, muscular man dressed in a loincloth and praying before a slightly bemused Boniface.

Indians in North America also shared mixed opinions regarding same-sex relations. In 1542, one explorer discovered a tribe in Texas that went so far as to allow men to marry other men.

In this century, sociologist Ruth Benedict noted that many North American tribes institutionalized homosexuality in what was known as the "berdache." A berdache was a man who, by his own choice, took on the dress and occupations of a woman. Berdaches married other men, were referred to as "she," and were genial social organizers. They had the best of both worlds: they possessed women's domestic skills and also learned to hunt and fish. They were often among the wealthiest members of the tribe, and the tribe as a whole benefited from their unique abilities.

This stands in sharp contrast to "civilized" European society where feminine traits, whether in women or in men who loved men, traditionally inspired contempt.

Christopher Marlowe

Playwright Christopher Marlowe was born on February 26, 1564 in Canterbury, England. As the seat of the English Church, Canterbury was an important and cosmopolitan city. Marlowe's experiences growing up there had a strong influence on his plays, most of which were set in cities.

Marlowe was only about two months older than William Shakespeare, the other great Elizabethan playwright. The two were acquainted with each other, and Shakespeare wrote that Marlowe had "a mightier pen" than he.

There are many differences between the two writers. Marlowe's works tend, first of all, to be more autobiographical than Shakespeare's. Marlowe's homosexuality, moreover, left him with little regard for women. In his *Dr. Faustus,* Helen of Troy is a shrew, and his characterization of Queen Isabelle in *Edward II* is far from flattering.

Marlowe left Canterbury to attend Cambridge University, where he was exposed to the ancient world's greatest literature, just recently rediscovered by Europeans. The sensuality of these ancient authors stimulated Marlowe, who had previously known only the writings of John Calvin and other Protestant

Christopher Marlowe: Tobacco and boys.

reformers. These ancient writings reflected a society more sophisticated than his own, and one in which the love of man for man was considered a subject worthy of praise in art and literature.

Marlowe became determined to express his own sexuality in his works. In one of his earlier works, *Dido, Queen of Carthage,* Jupiter is portrayed as being enamored of his beautiful cup-bearer, Ganymede:

> Come gentle Ganymede, and play with me.
> I love thee well, say Juno what she will.

In *Dido,* heterosexual love is at the center of the action, but the audience gets the distinct impression that the playwright's feelings are expressed by the queen, rather than by the male lead, Aeneas. Aeneas is called beautiful, and his lips are an altar for kisses.

In 1587 Marlowe moved to London and shared a room with Thomas Kyd, another playwright. They spent long hours writing together and, according to Kyd, they were lovers.

In Kyd's portrait of his friend, Marlowe appears as a rollicking Elizabethan rebel who enjoyed ale, tobacco, and barroom brawls. Kyd quoted Marlowe as saying, "All they that love not tobacco and boys are fools."

In religious matters, Marlowe was equally frank. He felt that churches were flimsy schemes used by the greedy to take advantage of the stupid. He was also convinced that St. John had been Christ's Hephaestion, and that Jesus had felt for him "an extraordinary love." While Marlowe was not alone in drawing this conclusion, it is remarkable that he was able to express this opinion without being punished for it.

One of Marlowe's most famous works is a haunting poem inspired by Virgil's "Second Eclogue," in which Corydon invites Alexis to live with him:

> Come live with me and be my love

And we will all the pleasures prove
That hills and valleys, dales and fields
And all the craggy mountains yields.

Another of Marlowe's more famous works is his play *Edward II*, in which that king's tragic gay love story is depicted.

In 1592, the Black Death broke out in London, and Marlowe left the city for the country estate of the earl of Southampton. The earl was young and attractive, and surrounded himself with young men who, according to his own description, had "full, firm-muscled thighs" and were willing to grant him favors. He also supported many artists at various times in his life, including Marlowe and Shakespeare. When someone suggested that the earl should marry, he rejected the idea as a "horrid prospect." When his family pressed him on the subject, he offered to marry any man they wished.

Shakespeare addressed many of his most beautiful sonnets to the young earl, though it seems clear that the writer's love for his patron was not physical.

Marlowe, on the other hand, loved and desired the young nobleman. In "Hero and Leander," he wrote of his feelings: "How smooth his breast was, and how white his belly."

Marlowe returned to London when danger from the epidemic had passed, but was killed in a barroom fight in 1593 at the age of twenty-nine. Marlowe's early death robbed the world of a body of gay literature equal to, or even surpassing, the works of Shakespeare.

Henri III

In 1580, the English ambassador in Paris wrote to Queen Elizabeth I, "The French Court is the strangest place you ever saw." He was writing about the court of King Henri III, who reigned from 1574 to 1589, and who was without a doubt one of the more colorful monarchs of the period.

Henri was born on September 20, 1554, the third surviving son of Henri II and Catherine de Medici. He was clearly Catherine's favorite, and at various times she called him her "all," and told him that if he should die, she would be buried alive with him.

There seemed little chance that he would ever be king. His father's health was excellent, and he had two healthy older brothers. But in 1559, Henri II was killed in a tournament. The eldest son, King Francis II, died of acute mastoiditis less than a year after assuming the throne. The second son, Charles IX, became mentally unstable, and Catherine ruled as regent through most of his reign.

Meanwhile, Henri grew into a beautiful — and a very conceited and effeminate — young man. Nothing pleased him more than being escorted on the arm of a well-built courtier. At a ball

Henri III: Mignons, but no heir.

given by his mother, Henri arrived in a jewel-covered gown, escorted by twelve young men wearing only transparent veils.

While Catherine was relatively untroubled by her son's behavior, others at the court were appalled. The Venetian representative, for example, wrote that the prince was "an androgyne who passed from Gomorrah to Sodom." The Spanish were equally upset about how Henri's behavior might reflect on the Catholic Church.

France in the late 1500s was the scene of many religiously-motivated civil wars, usually fought between rival Catholic and Protestant armies. Many Frenchmen were disgusted with a

Church they felt was morally corrupt, and Henri, as a member of the Catholic royal family, became a symbol of the Church's depravity.

Henri's gay behavior was only part of the problem. After a particularly good time, he would always go through a period of penance for his "sin," which often consisted of a public display of contrition. Sometimes he would lead a procession of the devout, dressed in a robe and cowl and beating himself for atonement. One of these processions turned into a strange spectacle with hundreds of men, women, and children dancing nude through the streets in the middle of winter.

Out of concern for the French political situation and for her son, Catherine bribed the proper officials and arranged for Henri to become King of Poland in 1573. He hated the place and didn't even take the trouble to learn the language. When his brother Charles died the following year, Henri joyously fled Poland immediately upon hearing the news, and returned to France to become king.

Catherine was happy to have her favorite son on the throne, and although he was only twenty, Henri was ready. He relied heavily on his mother's advice and that of the council she had formed. He also showed a certain amount of independence and military leadership, but he had alienated so many foreign powers with his behavior that his reign was more difficult than it might have been.

While king, Henri III waged bitter wars against France's Protestant forces. He was genuinely torn in his desire to solve the religious problem. Sometimes he followed his mother's advice, which was usually bad, and sometimes he tried to compromise to keep both sides as happy as possible. That usually didn't work either.

Henri's behavior also alienated many of his subjects. The people of Paris usually referred to him unkindly as "King of Poland and France by the grace of God and his mother, *concierge* of the Louvre, hairdresser-in-ordinary to his wife." Henri also formed his own "Sacred Band," called *mignons,* a group of young men of mostly humble origin who were well built, intelligent, and homosexual. Critics charged that they spent most of their time in palace dressing rooms doing their hair.

In a final attempt to bridge the religious gap in France, Henri declared that he did not intend to produce an heir by his wife (which was hardly a surprise) and named Henri of Navarre his successor. Navarre was Protestant.

That announcement ushered in a series of wars in which the king found himself in the unusual position of fighting with the Protestants against Catholic forces. Only after the Spanish Armada was destroyed off the coast of England in 1588 could Henri rest easier; Catholic Spain was no longer a military threat.

But if they couldn't get him in battle, they'd get him in the palace. In 1589, in the midst of a minor uprising, Henri was assassinated.

James I

James Stuart was born in Edinburgh Castle in Scotland on June 19, 1566. His mother was Mary, Queen of Scots. His father was either her husband, Lord Darnley, or David Riccio, who was both Mary's *and* Darnley's lover. A year later, Lord Darnley was strangled, and the queen was implicated in the murder. She was forced to abdicate, and the baby James became king of Scotland.

As James approached adolescence, these uncertain and violent beginnings, complicated by his baptism as a Catholic in a Protestant country, made his life more difficult. But the young king was fairly attractive, although he had not inherited the sterling good looks of either of his parents, and he was intelligent.

As a young man raised by politicians, James searched for someone to love and trust, and he found that special person in his cousin Esmé Stuart. Esmé traveled from France to Scotland in 1579. In James' poor and provincial country, Esmé's French grace and ease of manner were captivating. James called Esmé his "phoenix," and his "object sweet."

The Scottish clergy were shocked that their king was having a relationship with another man and powerful nobles forced the king to send his cousin back to France. He never forgave them for it. When he reached his majority in 1583 and was ruler in his own right, James seduced the son of one of these powerful lords, and then abandoned the young man.

At the age of twenty-three, James did his duty as ruler and married Anne of Denmark. He produced seven children by her — enough to easily secure an heir — and never slept with her again.

When his cousin Queen Elizabeth I of England died in 1603 with no heir, James assumed the throne of England as James I. His reception in London was cool, and this attitude changed little throughout his reign. The English disliked the Scots, couldn't understand them when they spoke, and had as great a dislike of homosexuals.

Nevertheless, England was wealthier and more refined than Scotland, and James experienced a degree of freedom he had never known before. He surrounded himself with young men, and became attached to two in particular. The first of these was Robert Carr. James was forty-one and Robert was twenty when they first met. Carr broke his leg at a tournament the king was attending, and James followed the young man to the hospital where he personally took care of him. The king fell deeply in love, and made no attempt to conceal the nature of their relationship. They exchanged deep kisses in public, and James often pinched the young man and fondled him between his thighs.

James named Robert Carr viscount of Rochester, and later earl of Somerset, making him the first Scot to sit in the House of Lords. His titles brought Carr wealth and power, and made him proud and arrogant. Eventually, Carr took another lover.

There are no records of James' reactions to Robert Carr's new love. Perhaps by that time King James had already begun his affair with George Villiers, whom he had met in 1614. Once again, James bestowed titles upon his lover, making him a knight in 1615, an earl in 1617, and a duke in 1623.

James I: Unseemly displays of affection.

James said that Villiers was his greatest love. When the Privy Council complained of James' "unseemly displays of public affection" for Villiers, the king who commissioned the famous translation of the *Bible* responded, "Jesus Christ had the same and therefore I cannot be blamed. Christ had his John and I have my sweet George." Thereafter, he referred to Villiers as his wife.

Unfortunately, George Villiers, like Robert Carr before him, showed little restraint in his thirst for power and wealth, never feeling quite satisfied with James' gifts. James seemed to have realized that his affection was not truly reciprocated, for he once wrote Villiers, "Thy dear dad always misses thee. Dost thou not *ever* miss him?"

James I died on March 27, 1625, and the doctors reported that his blood was full of "melancholy." The diagnosis has the ring of poetic truth.

Caribbean Pirates

If Robert Louis Stevenson had really wanted to make *Treasure Island* historically accurate, Jim Hawkins and Long John Silver would have been lovers. The pirate culture of the seventeenth-century Caribbean is the only known example of a predominantly homosexual community evolving its own set of institutions and way of life with little or no interference from the rest of society.

In the time of the pirates, European states were constantly at war. Between 1600 and 1675, there was complete peace in only one year: 1610. Most of the wars were fought for economic reasons, unlike the previous century when wars were fought over religious differences. Such a prolonged period of fighting caused severe economic hardship in many countries. The only job for many able-bodied men was to serve in the armed forces.

In England, that usually meant serving in the navy. In wartime, the Royal Navy required fifty thousand men. Their duty involved months at sea under dreadful conditions: the food was poor, sickness was rampant, discipline was harsh, and the pay was low.

The navy was an all-male organization. The only sexual partner possible for sailors between ports was another sailor. Despite the hardships, homosexuals found a haven in the king's fleet.

Whatever a sailor's orientation, the harshness of life in the Royal Navy caused many men to jump ship. But life on land was hard too, and many men soon longed to return to the sea. These men were most likely to become pirates. By the first decade of the seventeenth century, small groups of pirates had formed on the islands of Hispaniola and Tortuga to take advantage of the treasure fleets and trading vessels that passed by on their return voyage to Europe.

England turned a blind eye to the pirates' activities as long as they were raiding her enemies' ships. As a result, by the middle of the century pirate strength had grown considerably throughout the Caribbean. They patrolled the Bahamas and Bermuda, and had even formed their own society. One of their strongholds, Port Royal, was known as "The Sodom of the Universe." Antigua had a similar reputation.

Most pirates, however, were not very promiscuous. They formed close bonds with one of their comrades, their "messmate." These pairings were considered sacred unions, and the lovers were treated as a couple. Called "matelotage," this bonding had many of the features of heterosexual marriage, including the inheritance of property by one partner in the event of the other's death.

In his *Memoirs of a Buccaneer,* Captain Louis Le Golif wrote that two men bound in matelotage were disgraced if one of them strayed. At sea, if one lover was punished, the other was expected to share that punishment, even death. One love story told by le Golif was the story of George Rounsivil and his lover Timothée. Their brigantine was caught in a violent storm, struck rocks, and began to sink. Rounsivil searched desperately for Timothée, but was unable to find him in the confusion.

Caribbean Pirates: A society all their own.

Finally, deciding that his lover must have been in another life-boat, Rounsivil climbed into the last one and they pushed off.

When Rounsivil turned to take one last look at the ship, he saw the dim figure of Timothée waving to him. The others refused to risk all of their lives to return for him, so Rounsivil jumped over the side and returned to the sinking ship. The last thing the other men saw as the ship went down was George Rounsivil and Timothée in each other's arms. They became heroes for their love and fidelity.

Other members of the pirate society, particularly the captain and tradesmen, took teenage boys as their "lads." For the few heterosexual men on board, the smooth, small body of a boy was the closest he could come to a woman while at sea. Others were genuine paedophiles, and the relationships they formed were deep and long-lasting.

Women were sometimes captured and treated in a variety of ways. Black and Indian women, as members of darker races, were sometimes thrown overboard or died from neglect. They did provide some release for the few heterosexual men, but there is no record of a woman being kept on board for that purpose. White Christian women were treated with reverence and respect. They usually had little to fear from the marauding buccaneers, especially the threat of sex.

Pirate society was relatively short-lived. By the late 1600s, England had decided that law and order had to be maintained. The Royal Navy pursued offenders and many of those captured were executed. The lucky ones disappeared into legitimate occupations or quiet retirement, their matelot by their side.

Queen Christina

Christina, the future queen of Sweden, was born in 1626. Her father, King Gustavus Adolphus, was the Protestant champion against the Catholic forces in the Thirty Years' War. At Christina's birth, there was a membrane that covered her entire body, and no one was sure of her sex. She was also very hairy and cried loudly, and all the onlookers thought she had to be a baby boy. Throughout her life she was viewed as an oddity.

Christina grew to be a pretty girl with a slight figure, soft pale hair, and an attractive mouth. She did not, however, follow feminine fashion in manners or in clothing. She loved to ride and hunt, and swore constantly. Her mother once wondered, "Did I truly give life to a son?"

Christina's father was killed fighting the Catholics in the Battle of Lutzen in 1632. Christina became queen at the age of six, but did not rule until her eighteenth birthday. The Swedes were charmed by their new ruler, but Christina was not pleased to be queen. There was a world outside of Lutheran Sweden that she wanted to explore, and she knew that she couldn't do it while she remained on the throne.

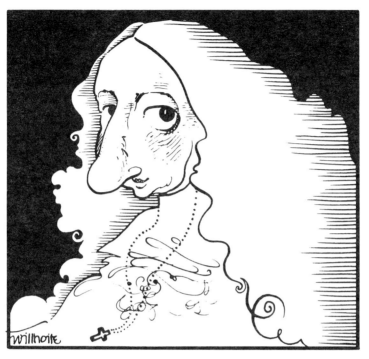

Queen Christina: She left Belle behind.

One need she could satisfy while she reigned was the need for love. In 1645 she met Ebba Sparre, whom she always called Belle. Belle became the queen's lady-in-waiting. Their relationship, which the queen made no effort to conceal, led to a great deal of gossip and speculation at court. Christina once told the French ambassador, "Belle is my bedfellow." The word spread over all of Europe, prompting Pope Alexander VII to declare that Christina was "born a barbarian, barbarously brought up and living with barbarous thoughts."

The queen of Sweden cared nothing about the talk. "I am condemned," she wrote to Belle, "to the fate of loving you always," often reminding her of "the power you have over me."

But Belle's love was not enough to make the queen content. In 1654 she voluntarily did the inconceivable: she abdicated the throne and left the country. Belle did not accompany her. For the following thirty-four years, Christina would constantly entertain and perplex all of Europe.

As soon as she left Sweden, Christina cut her hair and began wearing men's clothing. Everywhere she stopped she welcomed women into her bedroom. Her "masculine" ways were the talk of the Continent. In Paris, Anne Marie, duchess of Orleans, who had the reputation of being somewhat masculine herself, reported that Christina swore, slouched in her chair, stretched her legs in every direction, and generally "comported herself most wonderfully."

Christina eventually settled in Rome. Since the Romans had been exposed to all kinds of behavior for centuries, they tended to be fairly blasé. Christina could behave as she pleased without danger of causing a scandal.

Although her life in Rome was exciting, Christina never lost her love for Belle, and she was lonely at times. She once wrote that after having seen the most beautiful and charming women of Europe, she still had not met anyone who could compete with her lost Swedish love.

Christina's interests were diverse, and she indulged them all, dabbling in alchemy, collecting paintings, and writing. Her original writing project was a biography of her heroes: Alexander the Great and his lover Hephaestion, but she abandoned it in favor of a collection of maxims which included the saying, "All abandon us sooner or later."

On Christmas Eve of 1688, Christina, who was beginning to feel old and tired, predicted that her death would come within the coming year. Four months later, she died and was buried in Rome. One of her friends, upon hearing of her death, wrote a fitting epitaph: "She freely followed her own genius in all things and cared not what anybody said."

Queen Anne

Her contemporaries were some of the most powerful and splendid monarchs Europe had even known: Peter the Great of Russia, Charles XII of Sweden, Louis XIV of France. In a world ruled by men, in which women were usually consorts and playthings, Anne sat upon the throne of England from 1702 to 1714 and governed in her own right. She was the last member of the Stuart family to rule England.

Anne was born on February 6, 1665. Her father was James, duke of York, and the brother of King Charles II. At the time of her birth, there seemed to be little chance that Anne would ever wear the crown. But King Charles, although he fathered many children, left no legitimate heir to the throne.

After Anne's father became king in 1685, he revealed that he had been raised a Catholic. The Catholic Church was extremely unpopular in seventeenth-century England, and within three years James had been replaced on the throne by Mary, Anne's older sister, and her husband William. This "Glorious Revolution" led to the exile of James to France and left Anne one step closer to becoming queen.

Queen Anne: Surrounded by turmoil.

Like Charles, William and Mary failed to provide an heir to the throne, and when William, who had outlived his wife, died in 1702, Anne became the ruler of England.

With all of the political turmoil surrounding her, Anne grew up lonely and love-starved. In her portraits she appears to have beem plain, large-boned, and overweight. Anne was fairly intelligent and politically astute. But the one great drive in her life seems to have been her need for affection.

In 1683 she married George, prince of Denmark, but that did little to answer her need. George is best remembered by King Charles II's famous aside that he had "tried him drunk and tried him sober and there's nothing in him." George and Anne produced seventeen children, none of whom survived to adulthood.

In the year she married, Anne did find the love she had been looking for, but not from her husband. She met Sarah Churchill, the future duchess of Marlborough. Sarah was one of the great beauties of her time, and that beauty was complemented by intelligence and wit. Her greatest shortcoming was her fiery temper.

Anne and Sarah became involved emotionally, and Sarah provided the support that Anne needed so badly. Before she died, Queen Mary tried to end the relationship her sister had developed with Sarah Churchill, but Anne refused to let that happen.

When Anne became queen in her own right, she appointed Sarah Officer of the Stole; one of her duties was to attend the queen's bedchamber. The two women wrote letters to one another, even though they lived under the same roof, to provide a bit of privacy. From their letters it seems that their love, though deep and strong, was never expressed physically, except for an occasional embrace or kiss.

In these letters, Anne was "Mrs. Morly" while Sarah was "Mrs. Freeman." The names were more a way to preserve the illusion of equality than an effort to conceal the identity of the authors. "Oh my dear Mrs. Freeman," the queen wrote, "you can never imagine how sincerely and tenderly I love you." In another letter she declares, "If ever you should forsake me, I would have nothing more to do with the world."

Their relationship might have survived if Sarah had been content to be Anne's comforter, but she insisted upon becoming involved in politics. The queen was aware of Sarah's aspirations, but often disagreed with her lover in matters of policy. When Sarah grew tired of having her views ignored, she left the court.

Anne was extremely upset by her lover's departure, and begged her to return, but Sarah stubbornly refused. Anne continued to insist that Sarah leave politics to her, and a break became inevitable. In her need, Anne turned for support to Abigail Hill, Sarah's first cousin.

Sarah vacated her apartments in St. James Palace, asking only that she be allowed to store some of her belongings for a while. Anne responded that she could do so for a fee of ten shillings a week. Sarah responded by immediately removing everything, including the mantelpieces and doorknobs.

Anne lived three years longer, dying in 1714 at the age of forty-nine. During her reign, the English triumphed over the French, and their empire expanded. The prosperity and success of the period was later remembered in the phrase, "in the days of good Queen Anne."

Frederick the Great

One of the most powerful monarchs of the eighteenth century was Frederick of Prussia. The memoirs of his sister, Wilhelmina, which were published in 1888, tell the tragic story of his life.

In 1730, Frederick was a lonely young man of eighteen. He was handsome and intelligent, and was devoted to art, music, and literature. His father, King Frederick William I, thought these interests were effeminate and beat his son regularly with a thick cane to punish him for pursuing them. Once he had to be restrained by servants when they feared he would kill the boy. At meals the younger Frederick was not allowed to eat until his father had spit on his plate. Despite the constant harassment, the prince never reacted, something which only intensified his father's rage.

Frederick wandered in the palace gardens at night to find some peace. One evening he heard someone playing a flute, his favorite instrument, and he looked for the musician. That night he met Lieutenant Hans von Katte, the 25-year-old son of one of his father's generals. Katte had dark good looks, with thick black hair. It was love at first sight, and the two spent as much time together as possible.

The palace of the Prussian king in Potsdam lacked the sophistication of other European courts, where such a relationship would have been overlooked. The Prussians were an austere people, ruled by a rigid Protestant code of behavior. Frederick and Katte discussed the possibility of running away to find a place where they could be together and indulge their interest in the arts.

In October of 1730 they planned their escape to England. The prince was surrounded by spies, however, and as soon as they began their escape on horseback the king ordered troops to capture them. They were charged with desertion, a crime that carried the death penalty. They were then imprisoned at the fortress of Kurstrin, outside of Berlin, where they had separate cells, one directly over the other. According to the king's wishes, they were sentenced to death. When they heard the message, Wilhelmina wrote, they stood "without moving a muscle."

The king did not intend to kill his son, however. He ordered that Katte should be told that he would die alone within Frederick's sight. The prince knew nothing of this arrangement until the last minute.

A scaffold was built in front of the prince's window where, he thought, he and his lover would die together. Early in the morning of November 6, 1730, the date set for their execution, the prince was told of his father's plan. He begged for Katte's life, but his father refused to listen. Instead, following the instructions of the king, the prince was dressed in a plain brown suit and tied to the bars of the window in his cell, and was thus forced to witness his lover's execution.

Wilhelmina wrote that Katte slowly mounted the scaffold, turning when he heard Frederick cry out, "I am miserable, dear Katte. Oh that I were in your place."

Katte nodded, said nothing, and knelt before the executioner. He then looked at the window to see Frederick's face. His

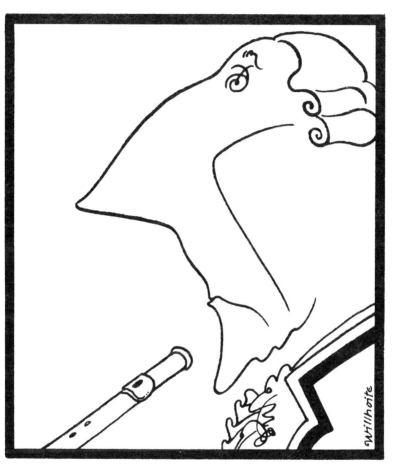

Frederick the Great: Forced to watch his lover die.

last words were, "Had I a thousand lives, my beloved, I would lay them all down for you."

Frederick fainted and could not be revived for several hours. When he finally regained consciousness, he refused to eat for days and cried continuously. Meanwhile, his father refused to remove Katte's body from the place where he had died.

Eventually, Frederick survived his father and became king of Prussia. He was successful militarily and expanded his country's borders, while liberalizing the Prussian code of laws. He abolished torture and press censorship, instituted toleration of all religions, and enforced the general education of all his subjects. He remained a bitter and lonely man, however, and died alone in 1786.

Colonial America

Although it isn't mentioned in history textbooks, homosexuality came to America along with the first settlers. These seventeenth- and eighteenth-century colonists were, by and large, a rough and lusty people, whose sexuality was an important part of their lives, and a major form of entertainment.

Since the earliest colonies tended to be overwhelmingly male, the likely practice of gay sex prompted colonial governments to make it illegal and punishable by death. Nevertheless, the first execution for "buggery" in Virginia did not occur until 1624, seventeen years after the colony was founded. There is evidence that this execution might have come about for other reasons as well, namely the greed of the victim's enemies.

Puritan New England, while showing more concern than Virginia about the sins of the flesh, also tended to turn its head and not notice when such "sins" were committed. Nicholas Sension was brought to trial in 1677 for homosexual acts in Windsor, Connecticut, but his activity had been common knowledge in the town for over thirty years. Once again, the reason for the trial seems to be revenge: the young man he was accused of sodomizing had been killed in King Philip's War and could not testify. The complaint was made by a former servant who held a grudge against Sension. Sension's punishment was light, however; he was merely required to put up his estate as a bond for good behavior in the future.

Another trial involving sodomy in the New Haven colony ended in execution, but the defendant's worst crime was that he had sown "the seeds of atheism, questioning whether there were a God."

Physical abuse — beatings, whippings and brandings — were the most common form of punishment for same-sex relations between men. Since women were not thought to have sexual feelings, there was no mention of lesbianism.

Although authorities tended not to give sodomites the maximum sentence, preachers like Boston's Cotton Mather routinely consigned them to "God's Hell," assuring his listeners that a love of "the sins of Sodom" could be cured through industrious labor.

Another of Boston's ministers, the Reverend Michael Wigglesworth, dealt with the problem not only in the pulpit, but in his diary. He felt ashamed of the desire he felt for his male students. At times he believed that God hated him, while at others he begged "Christ my husband" to help him. Eventually, he consulted Dr. Alcock, a Boston physician, who said that a cure, though difficult, was possible. He prescribed a "physick" to clean out Wigglesworth's bowels and advised him to marry as soon as possible. The day following his wedding night, Wigglesworth wrote that though he had "used marriage" his feelings remained the same.

Most homosexuals in Colonial America were in the same situation as Wigglesworth: closeted, avoiding the issue, praying for forgiveness. A smaller percentage were like Sension: secretly approaching others who seemed to be interested, terrified that one day someone might force the local authorities to act.

There was a small number, however, whose experiences were quite different. In 1703, Lord Cornbury was appointed

Colonial America: Discretion was a virtue.

royal governor of New York and New Jersey by his cousin Queen Anne. The governor spent every afternoon touring the village of New York elaborately dressed in women's clothing, and rumors flew about his sexual activities. He excused himself by explaining that his dress was a tribute to his cousin the queen, whom he supposedly resembled. The citizens of New York protested about this behavior to the monarch herself, who did not act (which is hardly surprising, considering she was in love with another woman at the time). Cornbury returned to England after serving as governor for five years.

With the more liberal ideas of the eighteenth century and the American Revolution, some statesmen did support the abolition of the death penalty for sodomy, although they still felt it was an abomination and should remain illegal. William Bradford of Pennsylvania, in a book entitled *An Enquiry* (1786), dismissed the issue altogether by flatly declaring that there were no sodomites in the fair state of Pennsylvania. According to Bradford, the youth of Pennsylvania worked hard and married early, thus eliminating the problem.

And, he should have added, they were very discreet about it.

Marie Antoinette

The French queen famous for her "let them eat cake" remark was actually not French at all, but Austrian. Since the French and Austrians had been enemies for some time, Marie Antoinette was never very popular in Paris.

She was born in 1755, the daughter of the Empress Maria Theresa, and one year later was betrothed to Louis, the heir to the French throne. Their marriage arrangement symbolized an alliance between these two long-hostile states, "The Diplomatic Revolution" as it is sometimes called. She became the focal point of hostile feelings among the French populace, and although the marriage didn't take place until 1770, Marie Antoinette arrived on French soil already an unpopular figure. She had to cope, moreover, with the immediate sexual advances of her father-in-law to be, Louis XV.

Adding to Marie Antoinette's public relations problem were her plain features and a protruding lower lip which, according to her enemies, reflected her disdain for all things French.

Her future husband, Louis XVI, was tall and fat, and uninterested in sex. His foreskin, it seems, was too tight for him

Marie Antoinette: Never a popular figure.

to have an erection, and he was unwilling to have a surgeon correct the problem. Rather than turning to other men, Marie sought out other women.

Her first affair was with the princesse de Lamballe. Lamballe was, according to all accounts, plain and unintelligent. She loved Marie Antoinette intensely, although her good sense told her that their love should not be too ostentatious or draw attention. Marie Antoinette gradually grew tired of her.

In 1775, a year after her coronation, Marie Antoinette met the duchesse de Polignac. Polignac was a strikingly beautiful woman, and from the time they met they rarely left one another's company.

The Polignac family was not as wealthy as they wished, and this eventually led to problems. The queen lavished gifts upon her favorite, at a time when the treasury had been greatly strained by the French defeat in a recent war with England. Furthermore, the French were giving aid to the Americans in their fight against the British. Consequently, the French people were heavily overtaxed, and some were starving. The princesse de Lamballe, ever loyal to her love, tried to intervene and make the queen see that her extravagance was making the problem worse, but Marie Antoinette ignored her.

Meanwhile, pamphlets in which the queen and the duchesse were accused of lesbianism were distributed in the streets of Paris. Rumors spread that the queen had been sexually involved with every prostitute in the city. Added to the general discontent against the monarchy, these rumors exacerbated the tensions that led to the Revolution.

The struggle began in 1789. Polignac fled to Basel, Switzerland, while Lamballe stayed at court. There she was captured and put in prison. In 1791, Lamballe was murdered, still wearing the ring that Marie Antoinette had given her as a sign of her love. Her head was cut off, and her genitals cut from between her thighs and stuffed in her mouth. The head was then placed on a pole and carried by a man who wore the princess' pubic hair as a moustache.

The queen, also in prison by this time, was forced to look at the head of her former lover. Two years later, Marie Antoinette was executed at the guillotine.

The Ladies of Llangollen

Few characters in our history are more interesting than Eleanor Butler and Sarah Ponsonby. One nineteenth-century magazine referred to them as "the two eccentric ladies of Llangollen." The two women boasted that, in the fifty years they had lived together, they had not spent a single night apart.

They were both born in Ireland of noble families. In eighteenth-century Ireland, women of their position either married or entered the convent. Eleanor, sixteen years older than Sarah, rejected both options. She had no interest in men, and when her family offered her a great deal of money to reconsider, she flatly refused. Sarah reacted similarly to the idea of marriage, and her family was not wealthy enough to offer a bribe.

The two women met at Kilkenny Castle, the home of Eleanor's family. Sarah had been invited by Eleanor's mother for a visit, and, according to their later accounts, they fell in love with each other immediately.

In the first moments of their love, they were having tea in Eleanor's sitting room. Sarah murmured that the room was beautiful and large. Eleanor responded, "My heart is bigger than the room and there's a place in it for you if ever you want

The Ladies of Llangollen: Poetry come alive.

it." Before the end of the visit, they concluded that they had been made for each other before they were born and that they must be together.

Their families were perplexed by Sarah and Eleanor's relationship, and unable to imagine that the two were lesbians, eventually decided that they had a romantic friendship.

Eleanor and Sarah wrote letters back and forth to each other in which they plotted their escape from Ireland. Eleanor, the more practical of the two, attempted to solve the problem of the money they would need to live. She realized that it would have to come from their families, since women of their station could never work for a living. One evening Eleanor informed her family that she was leaving and asked for financial assistance. They initially refused, but when they saw how determined their daughter was, they relented. They couldn't face the shame of having a daughter living in poverty.

One evening in 1779, Sarah jumped from her bedroom window into a flower bed below. Eleanor was waiting for her, and they hurried together to the garden wall. While climbing over, Sarah sprained her ankle, and they had to return to the house. One night a month later, they tried again. This time Sarah simply walked out of the first floor and out the gate. They walked as far as they could and slept in a barn. Sarah contracted an acute case of tonsilitis, and again they were obliged to return home. Their families were outraged because they assumed that the two were running away to be with men.

When they left for the third time, it was in daylight. They took a ship to Britain and settled in Wales, in the village of Llangollen. Just outside the town, they found the house they wanted to share, called Plas Newydd, and they bought it.

Although these two lovers lived in the country, they were in no way isolated from the outside world. They kept abreast of current events and read to each other from an extensive library. They entertained the neighbors regularly, and the hospitality was reciprocated. Even the local vicar called on them.

Gradually, the strength of their devotion brought them fame throughout Great Britain, and they received the visits of many famous people, such as Lord Castlereagh and Sir Walter Scott. The poet William Wordsworth called them a "living poem."

Eleanor and Sarah's love continued for fifty years. At least once each week they spent an entire day alone with each other. They would walk along country roads, talk, and sit by the fire reading poetry aloud or studying languages.

In 1829, at the age of ninety, Eleanor died. A little more than a year later, Sarah followed her. They were buried side by side in the local churchyard.

Emily Dickinson

Emily Dickinson was born in 1830 into an influential family in Amherst, Massachusetts. Her parents were strict, austere people, but her childhood, shared with her brother Austin and sister Lavinia, appears to have been a happy one.

Amherst was a small town, but it contained a college and was near the summer homes of Boston's wealthy intellectual leaders. Emily had a keenly passionate nature and a searching intellect. Living in Amherst helped her develop her mind and imagination, although sometimes she felt isolated and alienated from the outside world. This feeling increased as she grew older, and from 1861 to her death in 1886 she and her sister lived in their childhood home in a self-imposed seclusion, rarely venturing outside the house. It was in this atmosphere that Emily wrote most of her poetry, usually in letters to friends. She rarely allowed it to be published.

This mysterious nature has led to many studies of Emily Dickinson's life and poetry. There is no evidence that she ever had a physical relationship with anyone, but her emotional attachments seem to have been with both men and women.

Emily Dickinson: Her bride slipped away.

The first real love of her life was Sue Gilbert, a close friend of the family. When Sue married Emily's brother Austin in 1856, it's unclear which Dickinson loved her more. Emily remained strongly attached to her sister-in-law for the rest of her life, and Sue's marriage led Emily to a period of self-examination, during which she read Sappho's lyrics, Shakespeare's sonnets, and Thoreau's writings on friendship. A religious woman by nature, she studied the book of Ruth, and read of the love Jesus held for the apostle John. She also developed a strong attachment to her minister, the Reverend Charles Wadsworth.

In 1859, a woman named Catherine Scott visited Amherst. She was tall, attractive, and had a commanding presence. There was mutual admiration between Kate Scott and Emily Dickinson, and over the next two years, Kate returned to Amherst often. In April 1861, however, Kate wrote to Emily warning of the "dangers of our attachment," and their friendship began to cool, finally ending in 1866.

During the later years of her life Emily also developed a strong admiration for a Springfield, Massachusetts publisher named Samuel Bowles who made frequent visits to the Dickinson home.

Much of Emily Dickinson's poetry deals with romantic love, usually between a man and a woman, but often from a unique perspective in which Emily expresses herself from the man's point of view. In "My Bride," Dickinson writes:

> Her sweet Weight on my Heart a Night,
> Had scarcely deigned to lie—
> When stirring, for Belief's delight,
> My bride had slipped away—

This pretty and shy New England genius seems to have been confused by her attraction to both sexes. Rather than explore the passion she wrote about, she withdrew into herself and her poetic dreams. Fortunately, she left them for future generations to appreciate.

Susan B. Anthony

Susan B. Anthony was one of the great reformers of the nineteenth century. The New York *World* called her the Moses of her sex. Although she may not actually have founded the women's movement in the United States, she became its chief inspiration and symbol.

Anthony is remembered for her burning drive and strong character, but she also had a sensitive side. Her personal life, which revolved mostly around other women, was of great importance to her. She had a few male friends, but as a whole she considered men coarse and brutal. At age seventeen she wrote, "I should think that any female would rather live and die an old maid." Her opinion never changed on the subject. In 1870 she spoke out against "man marriage," saying that married life ought to be a luxury for women as it was for men. In 1880 she called marriage "legal prostitution." One of her goals for the women's movement was to show that living without any man's name was perfectly honorable.

Anthony's friendship with Elizabeth Cady Stanton was deep and long-lasting. In 1848, Stanton and Lucretia Mott organized the first women's rights convention in Seneca Falls,

New York. The Declaration of Sentiments, which announced the equality of women, was one product of that convention. At the time, such an idea was considered heretical; it was a man's world, as had been ordained by the Almighty. Women were naturally subservient to men and relied on men for their identity.

Anthony was excited by the Declaration and resolved to go to Seneca Falls to meet Stanton. She arrived there in 1851, and the two women took to each other instantly. While Stanton had a husband and two children and could not devote all her energies to the Cause, she offered Anthony her support, both emotionally and as a writer.

Anthony gained fame as a fiery orator, but she often was exhausted by the demands the Cause made on her time and energy. She had "weak moments" when it seemed the world was full of angry faces screaming at her from all sides. Stanton's home in Seneca Falls was a refuge for her, and she went there to find renewal in the daily life of the household.

The two women's characters complemented each other remarkably well, and the women's movement benefited immeasurably from their collaboration. Stanton was not a lesbian, or even bisexual, so a sexual relationship never developed. Furthermore, Stanton and Anthony disagreed over a number of issues, particularly the role of Christianity in the movement.

Eventually, Stanton's jealousy of Anthony's freedom placed an insurmountable barrier between them, although Anthony remained devoted to her friend, and she deeply mourned Stanton's death in 1902.

While Stanton was a friend for life, Susan Anthony experienced true passion with Anna E. Dickinson. Dickinson was a beautiful young woman when Anthony first saw her speaking out against slavery at New York's Cooper Union. They immediately became friends, and made a point of seeing each other as often as their schedules would permit. They communicated largely through letters.

By 1868, Anthony was busier than ever. She had founded

Susan B. Anthony: Marriage was legal prostitution.

The Revolution, a newspaper devoted to women's issues, and became its editor. Whenever Dickinson was in New York, she would burst into Anthony's office at the paper and cover her face with kisses. Anthony often urged Dickinson to move in with her, writing in one letter, "I have plain quarters — at 44 Bond Street — *double* bed and big enough and good enough to take you *in* — So come and see me."

Dickinson inspired a sensuality in Anthony that few would have imagined was there.

Even as Anthony grew older and the movement grew with younger women, she retained her position of eminence. By the end of the nineteenth century she had become a living symbol of the women's rights movement. Thousands looked to her for leadership and lovingly called her "Aunt Susan."

Anthony died peacefully in March of 1906 with one of her many followers holding her hand.

Sarah Orne Jewett

Sarah Orne Jewett was born in 1849 in South Berwick, Maine. Her formal schooling was irregular, but she did have a sensitivity to the beauty of the New England countryside and the richness of the region's culture.

Jewett entered the American literary scene during one of its most distinguished periods: Emerson, Longfellow, Lowell, Holmes, and Whittier had just preceded her. Further, many other prominent women writers were finding wide and appreciative audiences. Jewett and her fellow New England writers were strongly attracted to their region, and their works reflected this.

One viewpoint that distinguished women writers of the period was that they saw themselves as independent human beings, rather than simply shadows of men. When they formed relationships, it was often with other women, resulting in the term "Boston marriage," used to describe a primary relationship between two women.

Jewett had such a relationship with Anne Fields, a strikingly beautiful woman fourteen years her senior. Anne had married James Fields, owner of *The Atlantic Monthly*, at the age

Sarah Orne Jewett: Half of a Boston marriage.

of nineteen. William Dean Howells, the editor of the magazine, introduced Jewett to the Fieldses.

The two women gradually became intimate friends, and eventually exchanged rings as a sign of their devotion to one another. James Fields in no way objected to his wife's relationship with Jewett; he was dying and was happy to know that his wife would not be alone after his death.

After Fields' death in April 1881, Jewett moved into the Fields home. The two women built a steady relationship based on love and commitment. They enjoyed the sea and spent a great deal of time together at the Fields cottage in Manchester, Massachusetts.

They separated only when Jewett wrote. At these times she

would isolate herself in South Berwick and communicate with Anne through letters. The books that Jewett wrote often celebrated the love of two women, referring to it as "silvery webs that catch the flying heart." Unfortunately, Jewett's literary voice was stilled by a carriage accident she suffered on her fifty-third birthday in 1902. While she lived another seven years, she could no longer concentrate on writing without suffering dizziness. She had a stroke in early 1909, died on June 24, and was buried near her birthplace in South Berwick.

Herman Melville

In 1850, Herman Melville, at the age of thirty-one, was in the midst of a literary career that would establish him as one of America's greatest writers. He had already published *Fragments From a Writing Desk, White Jacket, Redburn,* and *Typee,* and he was working on what would be his masterpiece, *Moby Dick.* He was married and was the father of two children, a Victorian "man of substance," whose home life appeared to be a Currier and Ives print of stable conformity.

His writings paint a different picture, however. Melville is there, in the plots of his novels, storm-tossed, questioning, searching, with a morbid fixation on sin and redemption. And in each of his books there is always an eye of the storm, a calm young man whose purity and innocence are matched by a wondrous beauty.

In *Typee,* the youth has "rich, curling hair" with a "soft and beardless" cheek. In *Redburn,* he is the "Polynesian Apollo" with "large, black eyes" and "silken muscles." In each book the young man is masculine, yet something in his character softens him, makes him sensitive, and he seeks involvement with an older man.

Herman Melville: He found an older man to love.

In his biography of Melville, Edwin Miller says that the author's attraction to his "icon" was "deep and obsessive" and that there "is no denying the word 'love.'" Realizing the implications of this love, Miller adds that "it would not be fair to impute homosexuality."

Also in 1850, Melville met the man who personified his icon: Nathaniel Hawthorne. At forty-six, the handsome Hawthorne was also entering the most productive period of his career and was hard at work on his own masterpiece, *The Scarlet Letter*. Hawthorne, too, was married and the father of two children, but was a painfully shy man, whose quiet reserve unnerved many of his visitors. Where Melville was stocky, Hawthorne was slightly built, and fellow writer James Russell Lowell described him as having "a willowy body of nearly virginal beauty."

In the summer of 1850, Hawthorne was at his home in the Berkshire Hills near Pittsfield, Massachusetts. Melville visited the area and later returned to live. The two men met on August 5. Characteristically, Hawthorne had little to say about their first meeting, except to write an old college friend that he liked Melville "very much."

Following his own character, Melville effused over his new friend. In a review of Hawthorne's book *Mosses From An Old Manse,* Melville sings a hymn of praise not just to the book but to its author. In this review, published in *The Literary World* on August 17 and 24, Melville converts the timid Hawthorne into a magnetic personality with a voice "like thunder," who has "dropped germinous seeds into my soul." At another point in the essay, Melville goes on to describe Hawthorne's "wild, witch-voice that rings through me," and that he had "shot his strong New England roots into the hot soil of my soul."

For nearly fifteen months Melville and Hawthorne were neighbors. Melville, who had never been much of a letter writer, suddenly found time to dash off dozens of notes that were full of love, adulation, and erotic imagery. In one of these, Melville compares his friend to the Greek god Apollo "in all your beauty and power," and tells him that "your generous, melting heart has impregnated me." Also, in an age when the classics were much more familiar than they are now, Melville compares the two of them to Socrates and Alcibiades.

Melville burned Hawthorne's answers to these notes, but Mrs. Sophia Hawthorne described her husband's visitor in letters to her mother, which have survived.

Sophia Hawthorne, while puzzled by the relationship between the two men, welcomes Melville because he "appreciates very deeply Mr. Hawthorne's genius." Hawthorne, however, was more restrained. Sophia describes him sitting silently as Melville talks "in a great stream of words that dash waves of thought upon him." And she further states that even on their walks together, it was "Mr. Melville always seeming to be doing the talking."

After the Hawthornes left Pittsfield in 1851, Melville saw his icon only once again, five years later. Melville was on his way to the Mediterranean and interrupted his trip to visit Hawthorne, who was living in England. Once again, according to Melville, he and Hawthorne went for a walk along a beach. Melville did the talking; Hawthorne was silent.

Hawthorne died in 1864, leaving his admirer in deep sorrow. As an epitaph for this one-sided love, Melville wrote:

> To have known him, to have loved him,
> After loneness long;
> And then to be estranged in life
> And neither in the wrong;
> And now for death to set his seal —
> Ease me, a little ease, my song!

Walt Whitman

While some authorities have said that his attachments to other men were simply ties of friendship, Walt Whitman's poetry and letters indicate that the had strong homosexual desires. In fact, it is difficult to imagine how a study of Whitman's work could be complete without taking into account his homosexuality.

Born in 1819, Whitman grew up in Brooklyn, but as an adult lived in Manhattan, where he spent his most productive years. As a young man, he was robust, handsome, and slender, and often dressed in the clothes of a workman with a bright red bandanna around his neck. This style of dress was his way of identifying himself as a man of the people. Whitman was drawn to young working-class men, and this attraction finds its expression in much of his poetry.

"Adhesiveness" and "comradely love" were the words Whitman used to describe his feelings for men. The term "homosexual" had not yet been coined, and the existing terms for same-sex attraction all had negative connotations. The time in which Whitman lived was one of the most sexually repressive in history, a time when masturbation was believed to lead to insanity

Walt Whitman: Concealing his body electric.

because, according to one theory, semen and brain fluid were interchangeable.

Whitman experienced terrible pain in trying to come to terms with himself and with his attraction for other men. In *Live Oak With Moss,* a short collection of poems which he later broke up and divided among several other collections, he described his "Hours of torment" in the following terms:

> I wonder if other men have the like, out
> of the like feelings?
> Is there even one like me. . .?

Often, when he saw a beautiful young man, the realization that he could never act on his desires brought on what he called "horrible sloughs," periods of intense mental anguish.

There appear to have been moments when Whitman felt compelled to disclose his feelings, and it seemed to him that the only hope for alleviating his inner turmoil lay in public honesty. He never did actually take this step, however, and toward the end of his life he told a friend that his "secret" could never be revealed.

Perhaps the closest he came to public disclosure of his sexuality was in *Calamus,* a collection of poems which he began in 1856 and which, as with *Live Oak With Moss,* he later divided among a number of other collections. This group of poems has been described as the loveliest of his works. The following verses from the poem "Whoever You Are" show the extent to which he allowed himself in this collection to express his feelings.

> With a comrade's long-dwelling kiss, or
> the new husband's kiss.
> For I am the new husband, and I am the
> comrade.

In another poem included in *Calamus,* he wrote:

For an athlete is enamoured of me —
    and I of him
But toward him there is something fierce
    and terrible in me,
eligible to burst forth,
I dare not tell it in words — not even in
    these songs.

During the Civil War, Whitman grieved deeply for the millions of young men who were dying on the battlefields. He went to Washington and visited the hospitals to raise the spirits of the wounded soldiers.

After the war, he met a young man named Peter Doyle. Doyle was a horse-car conductor Whitman struck up a conversation with one evening. There was an instant rapport between the two men, and Doyle later said that it had seemed as if they had always known each other. The letters Whitman wrote to Doyle have been published in a book entitled, *Calamus: A Series of Letters Written During the Years 1868-1880 to a Young Friend.* They are in reality nothing short of love letters.

Edward Carpenter, who knew Whitman as an elderly man, wrote *Some Friends of Walt Whitman,* a short book in which he wrote of Whitman's theory of "the double life." Whitman held that the ultimate end of love was not procreation alone, but also the creation of "a new character" or "a new order of existence" which is produced when two people share a particularly intense love.

Whitman died in 1892, leaving behind a huge body of work, including his well-known *Leaves of Grass.* Although he never publicly declared his love for men, his poems testify to this love in some of the most beautiful language in American literature.

Ludwig II

Ludwig was born in 1845, the eldest son of King Maximilian II and Queen Marie of Bavaria, a region in Germany. Even in childhood, he showed signs of being unusual — his mother wrote that when he was six, his favorite pastime was to dress up as a nun.

As he grew older, he developed an interest in the German legends of Tannhauser and the swan-knight Lohengrin. His parents gave him a copy of the libretti to Richard Wagner's *Lohengrin* and *Tannhauser* when he was thirteen. At the age of fifteen, he heard *Lohengrin* for the first time and was completely overwhelmed.

In March 1864, Ludwig's father died, and Ludwig became king of Bavaria. His wealth and power were virtually limitless, and he became obsessed with the idea of using them to find Wagner and bring him to the court at Munich. At that time, Wagner was hiding from his creditors, and he was only too willing to go to Munich when Ludwig's agent found him.

After their first meeting, Ludwig said that he was in love with Wagner. Wagner, for his part, described Ludwig as beautiful, but never mentioned any deep feelings for him. The evi-

Ludwig II: He lived a Wagner opera.

dence seems, in fact, to indicate that Wagner was exclusively heterosexual. Nevertheless, he was an opportunist who understood very well that Ludwig's feelings for him could be of enormous practical value.

Ludwig set no limit on his generosity to Wagner. Besides settling all his debts, he provided him with a palatial home, a substantial income, and a new opera house. The royal family, the court, and the Church were all deeply shocked by Ludwig's behavior. They were convinced that Wagner was Ludwig's lover and felt that he was drawing too heavily on the royal treasury. Ludwig was strongly encouraged to marry and to dismiss Wagner.

Ultimately, Ludwig conceded, and Wagner was forced to leave the court. In letters written to Wagner, Ludwig proclaimed his love for the composer and offered to abdicate and join him. Wagner responded by urging the king to stay on the throne.

Not long after Wagner's departure, Ludwig agreed to marry Sophie, the sister of the Empress Elizabeth of Austria. He changed his mind, however, before the marriage actually took place.

Although Ludwig had a number of sexual partners, he seems never to have developed strong feelings for any of them. Rather, he continued to write long letters to Wagner, declaring his undying love and devotion. The nobility, ministers, and his subjects gradually started complaining that Ludwig was not carrying out his duties as king. He isolated himself increasingly and even considered abdication. Eventually, he became insane, living in a fantasy world inhabited by Teutonic gods and knights.

On February 13, 1883, Wagner died in Venice. When Ludwig heard of his death, he collapsed. Subsequently he had the body brought to Bavaria to be buried at Bayreuth. From then on, he neglected his duties entirely. By 1886, his family had decided that he could no longer reign, and Ludwig was committed to an insane asylum.

On the third day of his confinement, Ludwig and his doctor took a walk along the shore of Lake Starnberg. The following morning the drowned bodies of the two men were found on the shore.

Peter Ilich Tchaikovsky

Born in 1840, Russian composer Peter Ilich Tchaikovsky was a kind and gentle man. He was also quite handsome. His family doted on him, and his many friends loved and respected him. He was a successful composer with a comfortable life, but he was nonetheless tormented and unhappy.

Tchaikovsky was a homosexual and wished desperately not to be. He often confided to his diary that he would have given anything to feel desire for a woman and suffered throughout his life from his inability to do so.

After each sexual encounter with a man, the composer was plagued with profound feelings of guilt and wrote in his diary that it would never happen again.

Tchaikovsky wrote to his brother Modest, who was also homosexual, about his fears and feelings of isolation. In one letter, he wrote of his dream of one day finding love.

Despite his suffering, Tchaikovsky did manage to find some consolation in his music. He was fortunate enough to find a patron, Mme Nadejda von Meck, a wealthy widow living in Moscow. Mme von Meck wrote to Tchaikovsky, praising his work and offering him enough money to free him from all finan-

Peter Ilich Tchaikovsky: His wedding night left him in tears.

cial worries so that he could devote himself entirely to music. Tchaikovsky accepted her offer, and a longstanding friendship began.

Mme von Meck and Tchaikovsky exchanged a long series of letters, although they never actually met. In the seven hundred letters that he wrote to Mme von Meck, Tchaikovsky confided in his patron almost entirely, but he never mentioned his homosexuality.

Mme von Meck was aware of the composer's sexual orientation nonetheless and once wrote to him, "I must confess that just those things for which others blame you, I find charms in my eyes. Everyone to his taste." Far from finding comfort in her words, Tchaikovsky was horrified and his fears only intensified.

To dispel the rumors, Tchaikovsky decided to marry Antonina Miliukovea, a former student of his from the Moscow Conservatory. She was large and unattractive, and despite her education, possessed no real understanding of music. She was, moreover, an incessant talker and had a peculiar body odor.

Tchaikovsky married her simply because she was willing to be his wife although she knew of his homosexuality. It seems that she hoped to cure him. Tchaikovsky's friends made every attempt to dissuade him from going through with the marriage, but he was determined. The wedding was, in Tchaikovsky's words, "a ghastly spiritual torture," and the wedding night was even more horrible. The thought of joining his bride in bed sickened him, and he nearly cried at the idea of touching her body.

Their life together was miserably unhappy, and Tchaikovsky's friends eventually persuaded him to divorce his wife. Tchaikovsky felt incapable of confronting her, however, and one night went to the Moscow River with the intention of drowning himself. The water seemed too cold and dark, however, and he returned home.

When Tchaikovsky's brother and friends learned of his plan to commit suicide, they went to see Antonina, who did nothing but talk about the famous people who visited their home. Ultimately, she did agree to a separation.

After the separation, Tchaikovsky left Moscow for Western Europe. Antonina became increasingly unstable and was eventually committed to an insane asylum, where she died in 1917.

Tchaikovsky died of cholera in 1893 with his friends at his side. Witnesses said that he breathed a sigh of relief as death approached.

Victorian England

In 1885, the Criminal Law Amendment Act was presented to England's Queen Victoria for her signature; she read it and shook her head. William Gladstone, prime minister at the time, asked her why she had reacted in that manner. The Act forbade same-sex relations in public or private and seemed to him to be a reasonable piece of legislation. The queen explained that she understood that two men might have sexual relations, but relations between two women were impossible. The reference to women in the act was eliminated before the queen would sign it.

This story illustrates a common belief in Victorian England: that women had no sexual feelings at all. Sexual relations without a penis of some sort were inconceivable. Thus, all pornographic stories involving lesbian relations included a dildo.

One group did understand the female body and its responses, however: the female prostitutes of London. Though they earned their living through their relations with men, many turned to other women for love and genuine affection.

Other women also rebelled against the rigidity of Victorian society. Some of them acted out this rebellion by trying to

Violet Paget: Planning for the happiest generation in history.

behave like men. Among these were both lesbians and heterosexuals.

Harriet Grote, who was married to a teacher of Greek history, was called a "grenadier in petticoats." She wore men's clothes and sent amorous letters to the singer Jenny Lind.

Edith Chisholm, who like Harriet Grote wore men's clothing, spoke out for sexual equality and had several relationships with women. She may well have been bisexual, as she said that her happiest moments were in the arms of her husband to whom she had taught "the tricks of love."

One woman who seems to have been more radical than Grote and Chisholm was the writer Mary Ann Evans, better known as George Eliot. One of her admirers was the lesbian Edith Simcox. Simcox was twenty-eight when she fell in love with Eliot, who was fifty-three. At the time, Eliot was living with G.H. Lewes, a self-described actor *manque*. Eliot was not, however, averse to the idea of occasionally seeing Simcox. Simcox accepted the presence of Lewes, who seems to have been a voyeur, and called him a "brother worshiper at one dear shrine." After Eliot's death in 1880, Simcox made regular visits to her grave and tried unsuccessfully to buy the plot located at Eliot's feet.

Violet Paget, who called herself "Vernon Lee" was one writer who was unquestionably a lesbian. As she didn't have Eliot's talent, she never achieved the same degree of prominence. Nevertheless, she did gain some attention for asserting that if women were attracted only to women and men to men, the human race would certainly die out but that the last generation would be the happiest in history.

There were, of course, many women in Victorian England who were not fortunate enough to be able to express their sexuality. While young men could in many cases find sexual outlets, women, with very few exceptions, did not share this prerogative. Most women were denied knowledge about their bodies, but some women succeeded in discovering their sexuality nonetheless. Those who did went unnoticed since lesbianism was, in the Victorian mind, simply unimaginable.

The Cleveland Street Scandal

In the late Victorian Period, Cleveland Street in London gained considerable notoriety for a scandal that occurred there and that sent shock waves throughout English society.

Charles Hammond owned the house at 19 Cleveland Street. It was large, but unostentatious. During the day, it was unusually quiet, and the neighbors often wondered if anyone actually lived there. At night, however, carriages arrived and discharged their passengers who hurried inside the house. The visitors were without exception well-dressed men.

In July 1889, an official of the Central Telegraph Office discovered that some money was missing from the cashbox. An investigation led to the accusation of Thomas Swinscow, a fifteen-year-old messenger boy. Swinscow denied that he had taken the money, but when he was searched, he was found to have fourteen shillings in his pocket. Since this was a large sum, he was pressed to tell how he had obtained it. Swinscow said that he had earned the money by doing another job at night. When his accusers demanded that he tell them where he worked, he confessed that he went to 19 Cleveland Street where Charles Hammond paid him to go to bed with gentlemen.

It turned out that 19 Cleveland Street was a homosexual brothel for wealthy men. The police raided the house and found it closed and Hammond missing. The boys were taken into custody and questioned. As they came largely from the lower classes, they did not generally know the identities of the clients. One man they could identify, however, was Sir Arthur Somerset, the son of the duke of Beaufort. Somerset frequented the most exclusive circles of London society. He was a member of the Marlborough Club and an intimate friend of Edward, the Prince of Wales.

There was also evidence that Prince Albert Victor, son of the Prince of Wales and second in line to the throne, was implicated in the scandal. The prince was a handsome young man with a reputation for loose living. Prince Edward was informed of his son's possible involvement, which led to a great deal of distress on the part of the royal family. There had already been considerable scandal surrounding Edward because of his many affairs with women, and the queen and many others feared that the monarchy was in danger.

Prince Albert Victor was sent on a royal tour of India after which, it was decided, he would be married. The royal family denied the allegations that Prince Albert Victor had been involved in the 19 Cleveland Street scandal.

In the popular press, the boys of 19 Cleveland Street became symbols of the plight of the downtrodden who were being exploited by the upper classes. It seemed unjust to many that the boys should be tried and convicted for their actions while the upper-class clients escaped punishment. In fact, the public outcry became so intense that the Cabinet decided to take action. They issued a warrant for the arrest of Sir Arthur Somerset, charging him with "gross indecency with other male persons." Although he was far from being the only member of the upper classes who had been involved in the scandal, he was undoubtedly the most notorious.

Somerset fled to the Continent, and no effort was made to

19 Cleveland Street: Coming to life after dark.

pursue him. He died in 1926, never having returned to England.

Shortly after his return from India, Prince Albert Victor died of influenza.

Charles Hammond left England when the scandal broke. He eventually settled in Seattle and lived with Adele Gayet, a retired madam.

Lord Alfred Douglas

In the vast majority of accounts of the love story of Oscar Wilde and Lord Alfred Douglas, historians have devoted their attention almost solely to Wilde. Douglas appears only incidentally as the cause of the writer's fall.

The Douglases were the most aristocratic family in England. The father of Alfred Douglas was the ninth marquess of Queensberry. Alfred Douglas attended the best schools and went to Magdalen College at Oxford.

It was in Oxford in 1891 that Douglas, nicknamed "Bosie," met Oscar Wilde. Wilde was in Oxford visiting Lionel Johnson, who introduced him to Douglas. Douglas later wrote that it had not been love at first sight. He preferred men of his own age, and Wilde was thirty-seven at the time. Gradually, however, Douglas was attracted to Wilde for his sophisticated and artistic mind. They had their first sexual encounter six months after their first meeting.

A year later, Douglas wrote to his mother that if something should happen to Wilde, he would commit suicide to join him. His family was outraged. His father sent him a letter in which he called him a "perverted sodomite who has totally and utterly dis-

Lord Alfred Douglas: Always overshadowed by Oscar.

graced the family," and he signed it, "Your disgusted so-called father."

Douglas responded with indifference to his parents' reaction. He wrote poems glorifying homosexuality and even managed to publish them in Oxford's student magazine, *The Chameleon.*

In 1895, Douglas' father declared publicly that Wilde was a homosexual. Wilde responded by suing for libel. Douglas left England for the continent after Wilde urged him to do so, thinking that his presence in England would prejudice Wilde's case. The public generally assumed that Douglas had deserted Wilde.

While absent, Douglas did as much for Wilde as he could. He wrote letters to him, asking him to leave England. Wilde refused. Douglas also wrote to editors and journalists asking them to take up Wilde's cause. He went so far as to petition Queen Victoria, who did not reply.

The case was the *cause celebre* of the day, and Douglas followed its progress through letters and newspapers. The outcome, however, was for all intents and purposes predetermined.

At one point, Douglas' father wrote to him, offering him a large sum of money if he would renounce Wilde. Although he badly needed the money, Douglas refused, responding to his father, "I have nothing on earth to live for except Oscar."

As expected, Wilde went to prison. Gradually he began to blame Douglas for his suffering. It seemed to him that Douglas should have stayed in England and shared his disgrace. These thoughts provided the inspiration for *De Profundis,* a work in which he bitterly accused his lover.

Wilde was released from prison on May 19, 1897, and he and Douglas were soon reunited. They lived together for a short time in Naples, but financial difficulties soon forced them to separate. Wilde went to Paris where he died on November 20, 1900. Douglas was the chief and nearly sole mourner at Wilde's funeral. Shortly after Wilde's death, he told a friend that Wilde had been the only one who had recognized that beyond his body there was a beautiful soul.

For the following forty-five years, Douglas wandered, both physically and mentally. He married Olive Custance, and they had a son. Eventually, they separated. Douglas later converted to Catholicism.

In his later years, friends said Douglas looked haunted. He died on March 20, 1945. Near the end of his life, he was asked if he had anything to say. He answered by reaffirming his love for Wilde: "I have never known anyone to come anywhere near him."

André Gide

André Gide was born in Paris in 1869 to a devout Protestant family. His father, whom he loved greatly, died when he was only eleven, and he was raised by his mother, an austere woman. They moved several times after his father's death, and André, as a Protestant in largely Catholic France, never felt truly accepted in his country.

His Protestantism was not the only reason, however, for his feelings of difference and isolation. Gide felt an intense attraction to members of his own sex, and he did not know how to express this attraction. It was not until he met Oscar Wilde in Paris in 1891 that Gide began to deal with his feelings directly. Wilde's open homosexuality had a strong influence on Gide, who, after meeting the English writer, wrote in his journal, "O God, grant that my prison of morality may burst open, that I may live fully, and without fear, without believing that I am going to sin."

In 1893, Gide made his first trip to Algeria, where he first became fascinated by Arab boys. He spent the night with one of them: "a perfect little savage body, ardent, lascivious and full of darkness." He and his traveling companion also hired a female

André Gide: Living fully, and without fear.

prostitute, and it was then that Gide fully realized the pleasure and the implications of his gay encounter. His nerves began to wear thin, and believing he had contracted a lung ailment, he returned to Europe.

Two years later, Gide returned to Algeria and found that he had registered at the same hotel as Oscar Wilde and Lord Alfred Douglas. He almost left to find another hotel, but decided instead to stay and renew his acquaintance with Wilde. Gide was impressed by the two lovers, particularly by their openness. Wilde and Douglas made no attempt to hide their admiration for each other, or for the beautiful Arab men they saw on the street.

Gide spent the next few years in a state of confusion, searching for something that would restore order to his life. On October 8, 1895, he married his cousin Madeleine. Their love for one another was undoubtedly real, though not passionate, and throughout their marriage Gide continued to seek out boys for sexual pleasure. Madeleine was aware of this and accepted it for a time.

As Gide became more comfortable with his sexual identity, he sought to justify it in his work. *Corydon* was his landmark work that dealt with gay themes. He was fascinated by the inter-relation of sex, physical pain, and love. In *Si le grain ne meurt*, he wrote that love and physical pain are inseparable.

In May 1917, Gide met and fell in love with fifteen-year-old Marc Allégret. In the summer of 1918, Gide and Allégret went to England and stayed there through the fall. Madeleine was deeply hurt by her husband's action. Until then, she had always felt that, although she had never had Gide's physical love, she had always held the most important place in his heart. Allégret took even that from her. Although bitter and cool toward her husband, she was determined to make their marriage last. "I have had the best part of your soul," she wrote, "the affection of your boyhood and youth. And I know that, alive or dead, I shall have the soul of your old age."

Gide and Allégret remained close for many years, traveling together and sharing a special love for each other. After a long separation, Madeleine began to seek a reconciliation with her husband. By her death in 1938, the wounds had healed.

Gide became a world-renowned writer, and Allégret a respected film maker. Gide died in 1951.

Roger Casement

On August 2, 1916, Roger Casement sat in his cell in the Tower of London. According to the British courts, he was one of the chief instigators of the 1915 Irish rebellion known as the Easter Rising which, coming at a time when Britain was fighting for its life against Imperial Germany in World War I, made his treason especially threatening. Something else, however, made Casement seem particularly horrifying to the British: he was a homosexual.

Casement's homosexuality was common knowledge and assured that there would be no chance whatever for a reprieve. It also meant that he would be subjected to total disgrace and humiliation, as would his cause by its association with him.

The Ireland into which Casement was born in 1864 was a land which for hundreds of years had been dominated by England. Its people, most of whom were desperately poor, were despised and badly exploited by their conquerors. While Ireland fed England, the Irish themselves starved.

Time and time again, the Irish rose in an attempt to gain their freedom, but failed each time they tried. By the time of Casement's birth, though dreams of freedom still burned in

Irish hearts, there seemed to be little chance of their gaining it. The Irish were simply no match for the overwhelming might of the British Empire.

By the age of thirteen, Casement had been orphaned and had gone to live with relatives in Liverpool. In his teens, he worked at a number of jobs, and eventually took a position as purser on the *S.S. Bonny,* a ship bound for the Belgian Congo.

What he saw in the Congo horrified him. The Belgians' treatment of the Africans was brutal. They were seen as little more than animals valued for their labor, and they lived in the most appalling conditions imaginable.

The plight of the Africans filled Casement with pity, and he resolved to do what he could to help them. His first step was to join the British Foreign Service. In 1895, he was sent to Portuguese East Africa, now Mozambique, as British Consul. There, he developed a case of malaria and was transferred in 1898 to Portuguese West Africa, now Angola.

Wherever he went, he was appalled by what he saw. The Portuguese treated the Africans no better than the Belgians had in the Congo. Brandings, whippings, and mutilations were commonplace. The women were raped, and the men were worked to death.

Casement sent reports back to London describing in full detail what was going on and urging action. As he might have expected, nothing happened. In London, as in Lisbon and Brussels, it was accepted that the dark peoples of the world belonged to inferior races. White superiority was dogma that went unchallenged.

Throughout his years in Africa, Casement kept a diary in which he confided all his feelings regarding the horrors he witnessed. After 1903, many of the entries in the diary include accounts of his homosexual experiences. Contrary to what one might expect, no feelings of guilt or regret seem to have been attached to these experiences. In fact, the tone of the accounts is primarily joyful.

In Portuguese West Africa, he wrote about "Agostinho," whom he "kissed many times." Agostinho was one of several generic names he used for the young men with whom he found pleasure.

In 1906, he was appointed British Consul at Santos, Brazil. Once again, he encountered both horrible suffering and beautiful, dark-skinned young men. Like the Africans, the native peoples of South America were treated with terrible cruelty. On the rubber plantations of the Amazon River basin, the Indians were forced to work as slaves. In an account sent to London known as the Putumayo Report (1912), he detailed the atrocities committed against the Indians in restrained but outraged prose. He drew parallels between the conditions among the Indians and those among the Irish, whom he had begun to refer to as "white Indians."

Casement was intensely attracted to young Indian men and had a large number of sexual encounters with many different partners. While he enjoyed these experiences, Casement expressed a growing sense of frustration. Sexual relations with one anonymous partner after another was pleasant, but it left him feeling dissatisfied. In his poetry, he wrote that there was "No human hand to steal to mine."

A terrible tension developed between his private, inner self and his carefully constructed public image. Eventually, he decided that he would rebel against his heritage so as to remain faithful to his own true nature.

In 1914, shortly before the outbreak of World War I, he went to the United States on a speaking tour with the purpose of raising funds for an Irish rebellion. He arrived in August, just as Britain went to war against Germany.

Casement's sympathies lay with Germany, which he considered to be Ireland's best hope in its struggle against British oppression. He proposed openly that Germany settle the "Irish question" and went there in October to seek support for Irish independence. His efforts met mostly with failure, and he was

Roger Casement: A sensitive humanitarian disregarded.

taken at his own request back to Ireland in a German submarine. Upon his arrival, he was captured and sent to London.

Casement knew that he would be given a trial that would be mainly for show and that he would be executed, but he faced that prospect with remarkable equanimity. Death would bring him a martyr's crown and freedom from a life that was a "bed of thorns."

The trial began on June 26, 1916 and was completed in less than a week. The jury found Casement guilty of treason, as expected. He was sentenced to death by hanging.

The outcome may, however, have been different, had it not been for the diaries. They had been found among his possessions and put into circulation by the government, given especially to those who might be expected to call for a reprieve, seeing him as an Irish patriot.

King George V saw the diaries, as did members of Parliament. The American ambassador, Walter Page, after seeing them, wrote to President Wilson of their "unspeakable filthy character." They were discussed in the Cabinet where Casement was described as a "total degenerate" who was "unfit to live." Those who were responsible for the torture and exploitation of native peoples in the colonies had the luxury of feeling superior to Casement simply because they enjoyed having sex with women rather than men. In fact, it can be said that Casement's downfall resulted less from his political crimes than from his sexual orientation.

Rasputin

In 1916, Czar Nicholas II's place on the imperial throne of Russia seemed increasingly precarious. A feeling of impending doom was widespread among the aristocracy, and it was feared that not only the czar but all of imperial society would soon fall.

Many of the problems were caused by the influence of Grigori Efimovich, known as Rasputin, a name which translates as "dissolute." Rasputin had arrived in the capital of St. Petersburg in 1903 and by 1905 was received at the highest levels of Russian society. His piercing eyes and earthy sensuality fascinated the aristocrats, particularly the women.

Homosexuals were attracted to him as well, and Rasputin did not turn them away. His daughter Maria wrote that for him sex was a natural impulse and divine force that could be gratified by a number of means. Although he was surrounded by women, he also kept a private room at the Villa Rode, St. Petersburg's most fashionable gay bar.

Rasputin was little more than a curiosity until he met Anna Vyroubova. She was a lesbian and was not interested in him sexually. She believed, however, that he had the power to grant wishes, and she hoped that he would fulfill her wish never to be separated from Czarina Alexandra, whom she loved deeply. The czarina herself was not a lesbian, but she enjoyed Anna's devotion. She gave Anna a small house in the imperial compound at Tsarskoe Selo, twenty-five miles from St. Petersburg.

When Anna told Rasputin what she wanted, he promised that her wish would be granted. She returned to Tsarskoe Selo and encouraged the czar and czarina to meet Rasputin.

Rasputin gained a hold on Alexandra and Nicholas almost immediately. One reason for this was his supposed ability to control their son Alexei's hemophilia. In addition, Rasputin had a drink he called his "tea." He claimed it was a means to divine grace and that drinking it "made everything look good and cheerful." Rasputin gave it to Anna, who shared it with the imperial couple.

Rasputin's fame grew, and many wished to meet him. Among his many admirers was the homosexual Prince Felix Yussupov. Yussupov first met Rasputin in the summer of 1916 when the *staritz* ("holy man") was at the height of his power and influence. The first meeting took place in Rasputin's bedroom. Rasputin put his arm around the prince's shoulders and said gently, "If the czar and czarina obey me, surely you can." He gave the prince a glass of wine, which he called "the cup of life," and led him to bed. The prince felt a gradual paralysis come over his body as Rasputin caressed him. He then saw two rays of light come out of Rasputin's eyes and form a glowing circle in the air.

From then on, the prince visited Rasputin regularly. Rasputin called him his favorite disciple and "the little one." The prince, however, had a lover, Dimitri Pavlovich, first cousin of the czar. Pavlovich was jealous and, at the same time, was concerned about the power and influence Rasputin had over the czar.

Many others were similarly worried and wished Rasputin dead. The peasants, however, thought of Rasputin as one of their own and found comfort in the idea that he was close to the

Rasputin: Some people found him irresistible.

czar. Members of the aristocracy were therefore afraid that any attempt made on Rasputin's life by a nobleman would incite the poor to violence. On the other hand, if a homosexual were to commit the murder, it was hoped that the poor might not react in the same manner. For this reason, Yussupov was seen as the ideal assassin. He was openly homosexual and was intimate with Rasputin. And when the idea was suggested to him, he agreed.

The prince invited Rasputin to a party at his palace. That night, Yussupov played his guitar and sang Russian folk songs that he knew Rasputin loved. As he listened, Rasputin ate the food that had been prepared for him, not knowing that it had been heavily laced with cyanide. It had, however, no effect on him at all. Dimitri Pavlovich became impatient and shot Rasputin several times with a pistol, but he still did not die. Yussupov then beat Rasputin with a heavy club. Finally, they shot him again, covered his body with chains, and threw him into the river. When Rasputin's body was examined, the official cause of death was drowning.

The czarina demanded that the prince and Pavlovich be shot immediately, but the czar refused. He ordered, instead, that they be exiled separately.

As the aristocracy had feared, the peasants saw Rasputin's murder as a plot to remove the last link between the people and the throne. This belief combined with the scarcity of food and a number of other problems to bring on the revolution that led to the collapse of Imperial Russia in March 1917.

Rasputin's body, originally buried at Tsarskoe Selo, was exhumed and burned. To the revolutionary forces he represented the hated czarist regime. Before the body was destroyed, his penis was cut off and embalmed. It offers a further explanation for Rasputin's hold over some people: it was over a foot long.

Lawrence of Arabia

Thomas Edward Lawrence, better known as Lawrence of Arabia, is remembered as a dashing Englishman dressed in the robes of a desert sheik who led the Arabs to victory over the Ottoman Empire. He was born in England in 1888 and grew up during the height of the British Empire. The English at that time tended to be self-satisfied and had little interest in the cultures of those they considered to be inferior beings.

Lawrence differed from his countrymen in that respect. Other times and peoples had always fascinated him. While a student at Oxford, he immersed himself first in the Medieval period and then in the ancient world. It was through his study of the classics that he first came into contact with Middle Eastern culture. His first visit to the Middle East was as a member of an archaeological expedition, but he found he was more interested in the Arabs who were living there at the time than in past civilizations. Soon he began to adopt the Arab lifestyle.

In 1911 Lawrence met a fourteen-year-old boy named Salim Achmed (nicknamed "Dahoum") at Carchemish. Dahoum was sensitive and handsome, and Lawrence fell deeply in love with him. He made a life-sized carving of Dahoum in the

Lawrence of Arabia: Discovering a delicious warmth.

nude and put it on the roof of his house as a testimony to their
love. When Lawrence returned to England with Dahoum, their
relationship was hardly noticed. Because Dahoum was an Arab,
the English assumed he was Lawrence's servant.

In 1914 World War I began. Turkey was allied with Germany and Austria-Hungary, and the British realized that the
Arabs could advance their war effort if they rebelled against the
Turks, who had colonized Arabia. In order to gain their support, Britain promised the Arabs they would have a kingdom of
their own, and Lawrence was sent to be their leader.

The Arabs accepted Lawrence with little difficulty. In 1916, he rode with Prince Feisal out of Arabia to fight the Turks and even had his own unit. In his memoirs, Lawrence wrote with particular tenderness and admiration of the relationship of Daud and Farraj, two members of his unit. Daud and Farraj were both extremely handsome. They shared everything, wrote Lawrence, "with openness and honesty and perfect love."

In November 1917, Lawrence was captured while out alone on a reconnaissance mission. He was taken to the governor, a man named Nahi, who greeted Lawrence in his bedroom wearing a nightgown. Nahi asked Lawrence to make love to him. When Lawrence refused, Nahi tried to bribe him. Lawrence continued to refuse, and a guard was called. They seized Lawrence and slowly stripped him. The governor caressed his prisoner's body until Lawrence thrust a knee into his captor's groin.

More guards were called to tie up the Englishman, after which Nahi hit him on the mouth several times with his slipper. The governor then pierced a fold in Lawrence's flesh with a bayonet and rubbed the blood on his stomach. Finally, Lawrence was taken to the guardroom where he was whipped. He later wrote that after the twentieth blow "a delicious warmth, probably sexual" had surged through his body and made him relax.

The following morning, Lawrence was released, but his captivity left a lasting scar: it had introduced him to his own masochism. He wondered how it might affect his relationship with Dahoum, but he never found out. During his absence, his lover had died of typhus.

After returning to England, Lawrence's exploits brought him fame, and he became a celebrity. He grew tired of the attention and tried to re-enlist in the military under an assumed name. When his identity was discovered, it only increased his adventurous reputation. Finally, he legally changed his name to T.E. Shaw and enlisted in the army.

Meanwhile, he wrote his memoirs, entitled *The Seven Pillars of Wisdom.* Lawrence dedicated the book to "S.A.," which aroused a good deal of speculation. He never revealed what the initials stood for.

It is now generally thought that "S.A." stood for Salim Achmed.

Gertrude Stein

Gertrude Stein was one of the most influential writers of the twentieth century: her life and work had an enormous impact on such creators as Sherwood Anderson, Pablo Picasso, and Ernest Hemingway, among others. She changed the way they thought about their art, and they in turn changed the way we think about ourselves.

Stein was born in 1864 in Allegheny, Pennsylvania, now the north side of Pittsburgh. Her father and uncle owned a prosperous business, and their wealth enabled Stein to receive an education of a quality that few, and particularly few women, could have in the late nineteenth century.

She enrolled at Radcliffe and took courses under William James, the "Father of American Psychology," whose ideas had a profound influence on her writings. That they held one another in a special regard is illustrated by an incident that took place during James' final examination. On that day, the weather was beautiful, and Stein found herself unable to concentrate on her exam. Finally, she gave up and wrote "Dear Professor James, it is far too wonderful a day to write an exam." She signed her name and left. A week later when the papers were returned, his

Gertrude Stein: She and Alice (right) made quite a pair.

comment on her paper was, "Dear Miss Stein, I quite agree. A + ."

After graduating from Radcliffe and studying for a brief period of time at Johns Hopkins, Stein left America for France, where she lived for the rest of her life. In 1909, she met a native Californian who was visiting Paris on a cultural tour. Alice B. Toklas was drawn immediately to Stein's genius, and they formed a loving relationship that lasted thirty-seven years. Biographer James Mellow wrote that their love was "a marriage, and proved more durable and productive than most orthodox unions."

Stein and Toklas lived together in an apartment on the Rue de Fleurus. Their visitors were the great, and the near great, as well as their admirers, and everyone was expected to contribute to the discussions. It was a "salon" in the traditional French sense, where the mind was valued above all else.

Toklas always remained in the background, though not because she was not qualified to take part. Her chosen role seems to have been to love and care for Stein. Toklas, moreover, was the only person who could read Stein's handwriting well enough to type her manuscripts.

As the years passed, Stein became an internationally known author and intellectual figure. Nevertheless, on most afternoons, she and Toklas could be seen walking in a Paris park, immersed in each other's presence. Both in public and in private, Toklas called Stein "Lovey," while Stein called Toklas "Pussy."

During World War II, the couple moved to the country for a time, but returned to their Paris apartment after the Nazis left the city. It was there that Stein died in 1946.

Toklas lived until 1967, always maintaining that knowing Stein had been one of the few "authentic experiences" of her life. The two are buried in the same tomb in Pere Lachaise Cemetery in Paris with Toklas' name and date of birth carved on the back of Stein's tombstone.

Virginia Woolf

Virginia Stephens Woolf was born in London in 1882 into a moderately wealthy family. The household had a love of intellectual activity, and Virginia and her brothers and sisters were encouraged to make use of their father's large library.

Much of Woolf's childhood was unpleasant. Her mother's death from rheumatic fever when she was only thirteen plunged Woolf into a long period of depression. Her situation was aggravated by the sexual advances that one, if not both, of her half-brothers made to her.

In 1895, Woolf suffered her first attack of insanity. She heard voices and experienced an intense and immobilizing paranoia. These attacks were to recur periodically throughout her life.

Woolf emerged from childhood as a plain, insecure, and intellectual young woman who tended to form clinging dependencies, first on her sister Vanessa and her brother Thoby, and then on her friend Violet Dickinson. Dickinson was an attractive and intelligent woman who was seventeen years older than Woolf. They met in 1902 when Woolf was twenty and became strongly attached to one another. They traveled to Paris, and it

Virginia Woolf: Part of Bloomsbury's legend.

was Dickinson who cared for Woolf when her second attack of insanity struck in 1904.

In 1905, Woolf's brother Thoby, recently graduated from Cambridge University, formed a discussion group, or *salon,* made up of old Cambridge friends who gathered once a week to sit, smoke, and talk in an intellectual atmosphere that reminded them of school. This meeting usually took place at the Stephens home in the Bloomsbury section of London and formed the basis of what became known as the Bloomsbury Group.

The weekly meetings survived the early death of Thoby Stephens and came to include the two Stephens sisters, as well as the most creative minds that England would produce in the early twentieth century. Lytton Strachey, John Maynard Keynes, Duncan Grant, Desmond McCarthy, E.M. Forster, and Bertrand Russell were all members at one time or another, along with Virginia and Vanessa Stephens and their future husbands, Leonard Woolf and Clive Bell. Virginia Woolf wrote of Bloomsbury that "the majority of young men who came there were not attracted to young women."

Virginia Woolf's feelings for her new husband were of friendship and respect, not of physical passion. He was a source of security for her, particularly necessary during her bouts of insanity and at the end of her affairs with women.

The greatest love of Virginia Woolf's life was Vita Sackville-West, whom she met in 1922 at a dinner party. Sackville-West was a beautiful and intelligent woman, an author and a gardening enthusiast. She found Woolf to be an "incredibly lovely and fragile person," and wished to have a deep and primary relationship with her. This seems never to have materialized; in fact, it is quite possible that Virginia Woolf never had a physical relationship with anyone. Woolf did love Sackville-West, however, and the novel *Orlando* was her love offering. The character of Orlando, a man who becomes a woman, was based on Sackville-West.

Like Woolf, Vita Sackville-West was married. Her husband Harold Nicolson, a career foreign service officer, was homosexual. Nicolson and Sackville-West loved each other and had two sons together, but also pursued sexual relations outside the marriage.

Despite the fact that there was no impediment to their love, Woolf withdrew from Sackville-West after the publication of *Orlando* in 1929, and by 1934 their affair had ended.

In 1941, Virginia and Leonard Woolf left London to escape the German bombings during World War II. The war was Virginia Woolf's undoing. After the destruction of her home, Woolf felt another attack of insanity coming on. Rather than suffer through the ordeal, she wrote a goodbye note to her husband, and on March 28, 1941, walked to the River Ouse, tied a rock to her body, and drowned herself.

Willa Cather

Willa Cather was born in Virginia in 1873, but there was little about her that seemed typically Southern. She was plain, austere, and restrained. Like many writers of her time, she was deeply introspective as well. She struggled to come to terms with the industrial age and seemed to have one foot in the country and the other in the city.

Cather grew up in Red Cloud, Nebraska. She rebelled at an early age against her surroundings. She cut her hair, wore short skirts, and made no attempt to hide her disdain for tradition and convention. Her family was tolerant of her behavior, thinking that it was a phase that she was going through. Their tolerance was strained, however, when she asked to be called William. She further proclaimed in her high school yearbook that her favorite form of amusement was vivisection and that the greatest wonder of the world was a good-looking woman.

She attended the University of Nebraska where she discovered a love of writing. She decided that, in order to write, she would have to leave Nebraska to find the excitement, the intellectual stimulation, and the professional opportunities of the

Willa Cather: Her world had broken in two.

city. She initially chose to live in Pittsburgh, believing that it was "the very incandescence of human energy."

In Pittsburgh, she edited the *Home Monthly,* taught English at Allegheny High School, and met the first great love of her life, Isabelle McClung, the daughter of a prominent Pittsburgh family. Cather moved into the McClung home and was accepted as another daughter.

Although Cather loved McClung, she began to feel the need to leave Pittsburgh, which she described as divided into two parts: Presbyterian and Bohemian. When she was offered a position at *McClures Magazine* in New York, she accepted it and called her departure from Pittsburgh a "flight from drabness." Isabelle begged Cather to stay, and Cather begged Isabelle to join her in New York. Isabelle could not imagine leaving her home, so Cather left for New York alone in 1905.

In 1916, Isabelle McClung married Jan Hambourg. Willa was upset, seeing the marriage as a violation of their relationship. Nevertheless, just after her arrival in New York, Cather met Edith Lewis, also a Nebraska native, who lived in the same building as Cather on Washington Square.

Cather and Lewis did not experience love at first sight, but rather grew gradually to care for each other. Eventually, they chose to live together and did so for thirty-nine years.

As Cather grew older, she developed an increasing distaste for the twentieth century. She wrote that in 1922 the world had broken in two and "I belong to the former half." She hated mechanization and insisted that the apartment be lit with kerosene lamps. Disenchanted with modern life, Cather ultimately decided she would like to leave New York. Edith, however, enjoyed her work and had no desire to leave. Cather therefore resigned herself to staying with her lover.

In 1947, Cather died peacefully one afternoon while Lewis was away. Edith Lewis lived alone for the next twenty-five years.

Ernst Roehm

Adolf Hitler used the familiar personal pronoun "du" to address only one of the twelve highest Nazi leaders: Ernst Roehm, creator and chief of the S.A., the Brownshirts. Roehm is also distinguished by the fact that, of those twelve, he was the only known homosexual.

After losing the First World War, the imperial government and the economy of Germany were in a desperate state. A quasi-republican government was set up, but it failed to gain the confidence of the German people. Millions of former soldiers traveled from city to city looking for work. A number of these joined the Communists who hoped to spread revolution from Russia to Germany. Others joined paramilitary units known as *Freikorps* whose primary goal was to destroy communism.

Roehm was a member of the *Freikorps* and served with them in Munich where he met Hitler. The future *fuehrer* of the Third Reich had become involved with the National Socialist German Workers Party — the Nazis. At the time, there were only twenty members.

Roehm was mesmerized by Hitler's powerful personality. At the same time, Hitler recognized Roehm's drive, his abilities,

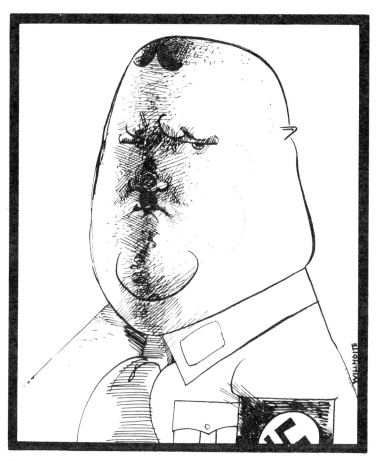

Ernst Roehm: Lining up on the wrong side.

and his complete lack of scruples. The two men agreed that the best means to attain political power was through force. They saw the party's need for a military branch.

In 1921 Roehm organized the S.A. in response to this need. He modeled his army on Italian dictator Benito Mussolini's Blackshirts, and the troops were recruited from the *lumpen proletariet,* the dregs of society. Roehm trained them to be brutal, and they became the party's strength.

The Nazis made their first attempt at violent revolution in 1923 in the Munich *Putsch* when they tried to overthrow the Bavarian government. The attempt failed, and Hitler was sent to Landberg Prison. This setback led Hitler to the decision to use legal means to gain power.

Throughout this time, Roehm indulged regularly in homosexual activity, and it seems that Hitler was aware of his colleague's behavior. Hitler was generally prudish regarding sexual matters, but was willing in Roehm's case to overlook this irregularity.

The other Nazi leaders, however, were outraged, especially when Roehm brought charges of theft against a male prostitute he had engaged for the night. Goebbles and Himmler urged Hitler to dismiss Roehm, but Hitler refused to do so.

Roehm remained in Germany until 1925, at which time Hitler did finally ask him to leave. Hitler's decision was not based, however, on Roehm's sexual activity, but on the fact that Roehm was a man of violence whose membership in the party would be damaging to its image of legal respectability.

Roehm went to Bolivia where he was miserably unhappy. He wrote to Hitler and to others begging to be allowed to return to Germany. In 1930 Hitler asked Roehm to return to Germany to again lead the S.A.

Roehm continued to express his sexuality openly and was accompanied at all times by handsome young men. He also conducted orgies in his home.

Himmler and other Nazi leaders complained regularly to

Hitler about Roehm's behavior. Accounts of his activities began to appear in the party-controlled press, and Hitler called it a smear campaign. The leaders of the party became increasingly disturbed at reports that Roehm was planning "the real revolution to come." They were unsure of what Roehm intended, but they had little reason to doubt that Roehm, with his army of perfectly disciplined and loyal soldiers, was capable of committing unimaginable atrocities.

In April 1934, Hitler met with his generals and reached an agreement with them in which the army offered its unconditional support to Hitler in return for Roehm's dismissal.

On the night of June 29, 1934, Roehm held a party at his lodge at Bad Wiessee near Munich. The following morning units of the Gestapo surrounded the house, and Hitler and his lieutenants arrested Roehm and his guests. Many were shot immediately. Roehm was sent to Stadelheim Prison in Munich. On July 1, Hitler approved Roehm's execution. Roehm was shot in his cell and died murmuring "Mein Fuehrer."

The execution was explained as an attack against homosexuality. Radio Berlin announced that "from a moral point of view, there was no room for pity." Hitler was portrayed as a righteous leader who had saved the nation from iniquity.

Three years after Roehm's death, Hitler was asked to comment on him. The *fuehrer* responded by saying that Roehm would always be remembered as the second man after himself in the history of the Nazis.

Pink Triangles

The "Gay Holocaust" took place at Dachau, Buchenwald, Sachsenhausen, and Flossenburg. Homosexuals were sent to these and to other camps to work and to die. Just a few years earlier, many people had been living openly homosexual lifestyles, although homosexuality was technically a crime. Few of those who were openly gay realized that they were living with a false sense of security and that soon the relatively relaxed atmosphere would end with the rise of the Nazis.

At Dachau there is a long concrete platform with five steel posts where eight homosexuals were hung one Christmas Eve. The eight men were four pairs of lovers. They were strung up by their necks, two to a post. They were deliberately hung just out of reach of each other, so that they could see the other's suffering, but could not offer a consoling touch. In front of the platform, a Christmas tree had been set up, and the other homosexual prisoners were forced to stand in front of it and sing Christmas carols while their comrades died.

Heinrich Himmler, chief of the SS and of the Gestapo, believed that there was a "Homosexual Question" just as there was a "Jewish Question." According to his thinking, homosex-

Pink Triangles: Never forget.

uals were alien beings, a third sex, and not really human. This would explain why they were different from the majority, and particularly why there seemed to be so many geniuses among them. Himmler further maintained that homosexuals were organized in a conspiracy to take over the world through a secret "Order of the Third Sex." For this reason, it was necessary to exterminate them.

In 1933, Department II of the Gestapo was set up with the express purpose of hunting down and imprisoning homosexuals. Thousands were arrested and sent to Dachau and other camps. They were forced to wear a pink triangle, which singled them out for especially severe brutality.

Upon arrival in the camps, homosexuals were forced to strip and to yell, "I am a faggot, sir." Then they were shaved, given a number, and told that, when they were addressed, they should always answer, for example, "Queer 4567."

If two men were known to be lovers, they were made to watch as one or the other was raped by the guards. Afterwards, they were often clubbed to death or attacked by dogs who had been trained to go for the genitals.

For the homosexual survivors of the camps, there was no compensation. In fact, the sufferings of the homosexual victims of the Nazis were largely forgotten after the war. Hitler's statute outlawing homosexuality remained on the books in West Germany until 1969.

Eleanor Roosevelt

Eleanor Roosevelt was born in 1884 to a wealthy New York family. As a child she was lonely, shy, and awkward. In 1902 she met her cousin Franklin Delano Roosevelt who was handsome and athletic. In 1905 they were married.

It is unlikely that Eleanor ever felt passionate love for F.D.R. Many years into their marriage, Eleanor Roosevelt wrote that "it seemed the thing to do," and that it was only much later that she found out what loving really was. The evidence seems to indicate that it was not her husband that she learned to love, although the births of their five children give evidence of a continuing sexual relationship.

From 1905 to 1918 she conformed to the role that society expected of her. She then discovered letters that her secretary Lucy Mercer had written to F.D.R. which clearly showed that they were having an affair. The revelation changed Eleanor's outlook entirely. She agreed to remain married to her husband under the conditions that Mercer would be dismissed and that all physical relations between her husband and herself would end. To protect his political career, F.D.R. agreed.

Eleanor Roosevelt: She and FDR made a deal.

From that time on, Eleanor rejected the traditional role of wife and mother. She became increasingly independent and aware of herself as an individual who neither needed nor wanted a man to define her or to meet her emotional needs.

Gradually Eleanor Roosevelt developed deep feelings of respect and friendship for her husband, though she also began to look to other women for emotional fulfillment. Throughout her life, Eleanor found that women evoked the strongest response in her, although she did have many friendships with men.

In 1924 she met Nancy Cook and Marion Dickerman, two women who shared an apartment in Greenwich Village. The three women became close friends, and in 1925 they decided to make a home together at the Roosevelt family estate at Hyde Park. F.D.R. gave his consent, and they built a house which they called Val-Kill Cottage. F.D.R. referred to it as the "love nest on the Val-Kill."

Cook and Dickerman established their regular residence there, and Eleanor spent as much time with them as her schedule allowed. The three women had picnics together, read to each other, and had long conversations. While it is certain that Cook and Dickerman's relationship had a sexual aspect, Eleanor remained somewhat detached.

In 1932 Eleanor met Lorena Hickok, the woman who would be the great love of her life. F.D.R. was the governor of New York and the Democratic nominee for the presidency, and the Associated Press had assigned Hickok to cover the Roosevelts.

Eleanor handled herself well throughout the campaign, but was far from elated when her husband was elected. Her fears and insecurities made her dread the role of First Lady. Hickok offered her support, which Eleanor accepted, inviting her friend to move into the White House.

There has been an enormous amount of debate regarding the nature of their relationship. The letters they wrote to each other, however, leave little doubt regarding this question: Eleanor Roosevelt and Hickok loved each other passionately.

F.D.R. died in April 1945. After his death, Eleanor continued to be a prominent international figure. When Eleanor died in 1962, she was buried beside her husband at Hyde Park. Hickok could not attend the funeral, but she did visit the cemetery with a local minister some time later. Arthritis prevented her from actually reaching the grave, so the minister left the sprig of dried goldenrod that she had brought.

Joseph McCarthy

Joe McCarthy, a senator from Wisconsin in the 1950s, made his political fortune preaching anti-communism. He claimed that the communists were responsible for what was wrong in America, and many people chose to believe him.

In 1950, the United States — the country that had led the allied forces to victory over Germany and Japan — was no longer the unchallenged leader of the world. The Marxist government of the Soviet Union offered a different approach to the rebuilding of the world's economy, and Soviet leader Joseph Stalin was intent on spreading the communist ideal.

Americans reacted with panic, and McCarthy took advantage of that panic by claiming that subversive elements within the U.S. were weakening the nation and allowing the Soviet Union to succeed in conquering the world. He accused artists and intellectuals of being communists and said he even knew of communists who worked for the State Department.

McCarthy also believed that homosexuals were communists. When gays organized and formed the Mattachine Society, McCarthy claimed that Stalin was president of the society, and that this "Homintern" was as much a part of his plan for world

Joseph McCarthy: Throwing stones from a glass house.

conquest as was the Comintern, the world-wide organization of communist parties.

Though McCarthy's claims had no basis in reality, they caught on and became a national cause. In 1953 the State Department published a report in which it claimed to have discovered and fired "531 perverts." This action was in line with a report approved by the Senate which had stated, "There is no place in the United States Government for persons who violate the accepted standards of morality."

President Eisenhower followed suit by issuing an Executive Order banning from government jobs "all persons guilty of sexual perversion." Meanwhile, in the Senate, McCarthy was advocating the extermination of all "homos," while one of his colleagues supported the idea of creating detention camps for "Communist perverts."

The anti-homosexual campaign in Washington had a strong impact throughout the country. In Boise, Idaho, for example, a campaign of abuse was waged against gays, in which persons suspected of homosexuality were systematically harassed and persecuted. An order of the town council which called for a cleanup of all homosexuals led to the arrest of 1,472 men. In a city of 100,000, that figure is especially shocking. Even more shocking is the fact that not one political group objected to such acts of persecution.

No one dared. McCarthy was too popular and the public fear too strong. Even President Eisenhower wouldn't challenge his fellow Republican. McCarthy's undoing finally came about as a result of his televised Senate hearings in 1954. When the public was presented with the senator's methods in their own living rooms, enthusiasm for his witch hunt died down. Seven months later, McCarthy was censured for conduct unbecoming a U.S. senator. Although his campaign was over, McCarthy left behind hundreds of ruined reputations and a number of suicides. He also established a link in the public mind between homosexuality and subversion.

Perhaps the most pathetic part of this tragedy is that both McCarthy and his chief counsel, Roy Cohn, were homosexual. Columnist Drew Pearson speculated on the possibility as early as 1952, and others have confirmed it since. McCarthy died in 1957 of "acute hepatitis, cause unknown."

Cohn, who appeared at McCarthy's side during the Senate hearings, repeatedly denied his homosexuality until his death from AIDS in 1986. A friend of Cohn, columnist William Safire, wrote that Cohn "denied his homosexuality because he could never reconcile it with his self-image of political masculinity."

James Dean

In the fifties, many Americans hoped that through conformity they could find stability and security, and the nation dedicated itself to the pursuit of sameness. Many young people, however, longed for individualism and rebellion. They saw these qualities in the performances of homosexual film stars such as Montgomery Clift, Nick Adams, Sal Mineo, and, above all, James Dean.

James Dean possessed what one critic called a "brilliant vulnerability." He projected the image of a beautiful and disturbed young man whose capacity to love left him defenseless. Dean was almost the personification of the idea of rebellion.

He arrived in Hollywood from the Actors Studio in New York. His first lover was Rogers Brackett, a television director. Their relationship was presented to the public as that of a father and son, though this was hardly the case.

Dean himself claimed to be bisexual. Kenneth Angers wrote in *Hollywood Babylon II,* however, that Dean was in fact exclusively homosexual. Hedda Hopper once asked Dean how he had avoided the draft, and Dean responded, "I kissed the medic." This story may be apocryphal, but, according to all ac-

James Dean: He kissed the medic.

counts, Dean did avoid the draft by admitting he was gay. If this
is true, it was a startling act of defiance. At that time, an admis-
sion of homosexuality was unheard of.

Dean was seen regularly at The Club, an East Hollywood
leather bar. The other customers referred to him as the "human
ashtray" because he took pleasure in having people put out their
cigarettes on his chest. At his death, the coroner noted in his
report that Dean's torso was covered with a "constellation of
kerotoid scars."

Dean's personality was far more complex than such stories

suggest. Beyond his self-destructive tendencies and macho image was an extreme sensitivity. Elizabeth Weis in *The Movie Star* describes him as "wounded with the luminous expression of a child longing for love." The description seems to have been apt.

Dean made three films: *Rebel Without a Cause, Giant,* and *East of Eden.* All of them explore themes of angst and the search for love. Much of Dean's appeal was due to the impression he gave of being tormented and of having a deep need for love. Young people identified with his pain, even if they were ignorant of its true cause.

It was unthinkable that Dean's homosexuality should be revealed to the public. Nevertheless, it is not difficult to sense sexual tension between Dean and Mineo in *Rebel Without a Cause,* which adds greatly to the emotional power of the film.

Dean died in an automobile accident in 1955 at the age of twenty-four. There was an enormous outpouring of grief on the part of the American public. Eight hundred thousand people paid twenty-five cents each to see the wreck of the car. Some fans even went so far as to commit suicide in response to his death. The fact that mail continues to be addressed to him today, more than thirty years after his death, attests to the enormous impact he had on American society.

Christopher Isherwood

Christopher Isherwood made conscious decisions about the kind of life he wanted to live, and he refused to accept life on any terms other than his own. In *Christopher and His Kind,* he wrote, "My will is to live according to my nature."

The fact that Isherwood died only recently makes it difficult to determine his ultimate significance and influence. Somerset Maugham called him "the hope of English fiction." Others believe he was a sort of prophet or avatar in homosexual history.

Isherwood was brilliant and articulate, and he was in revolt, not against his own homosexuality, but against those who tried to make him deny his true self. He refused to accept the will of the majority as a standard for his life. Rather, he spent much of his life fighting against what he called the "heterosexual dictatorship."

He was born on August 26, 1904 to an upper-class English family. His father was in the military and was killed in World War I. Isherwood attended private school and went to Cambridge University. It was in Cambridge that he had his first homosexual encounter.

Christopher Isherwod: Living according to his nature.

After the war, he left England to live in Berlin, which was then the gay capital of Europe. While there, he met a vast number of men and had many one-night stands as well as long-lasting relationships.

Besides the exciting aspects of homosexual life, he began to discover the other side of the homosexual experience: alienation, loneliness, and suffering. This led him to write about the homosexual man who stood alone with no family, no home, no country, and no religion. He recognized the particular difficulty of the homosexual experience: whereas a black or a Jewish person could find support in his family, the homosexual ordinarily came from a heterosexual family and was therefore alone. Isherwood saw this state of aloneness as a common bond that linked homosexuals.

At the approach of World War II, Isherwood left Europe with the poet W.H. Auden. They went first to the Far East and then to America, which both later made their home. This was also the beginning of the period in which Isherwood wrote his finest works.

Isherwood often spoke of finding an ideal companion. In 1938 he told the writer George Davis that this man would be eighteen, blond, intelligent, and would have sexy legs. In 1953, at the age of forty-seven, Isherwood met Don Bachardy, who seemed to fit this description perfectly. Their friends reacted, for the most part, with dismay and found it hard to imagine that the relationship could last.

The relationship did last, however, for over thirty years and proved to be an invaluable source of creative energy for both men. In the last decades of his life, Isherwood's writings became even more affirmatively gay than they had been before. Although he may have continued to believe that gay men were condemned to a certain degree of alienation, he could no longer say that they had no place. He had found a home, a country, and a life's companion. Further, his revolt against heterosexual oppression lent substance and purpose to his life. Perhaps the most important lesson of his life was that to be in rebellion *for,* rather than against, oneself leads to strength, pride, and a rich and satisfying life.

For Further Reading

"The Ancient World"
History Begins in Sumer, by S.N. Kramer
A Problem in Greek Ethics, by John Addington Symonds

"Akhenaten"
Akhenaten: the Heretic King, by Donald Redford
Ikhnaton: Legend and History, by F.J. Giles

"David and Jonathan"
Holy Bible, I Samuel

"Sappho"
Love Songs of Sappho, by Paul Roche
Sappho's Island, by Joseph Braddock

"The Sacred Band"
The Theban Hegemony, by John Buckler
The Will of Zeus, by Stringfellow Barr

"Alcibiades"
The Magnificent Traitor, by Lynn and Gray Poole
The Symposium of Plato

"Alexander the Great"
The Search for Alexander, by Robin Lane Fox
Lives of the Noble Greeks and Romans, by Plutarch

"Hadrian"
Beloved and God, by Royston Lambert
Sex in History, by G. Rattray Taylor

"Elagabalus"
The Young Emperors, by George C. Brauer
The Rise and Fall of the Roman Empire, by Edward Gibbon

"Jesus of Nazareth"
Holy Bible, The Gospel of Mark
Holy Bible, The Gospel of John

"The Church"
Book of Gomorrah, by Peter Damian
Sexual Practices and the Medieval Church, edited by
     Vern L. Bullough and James Brundage

"The Popes"
Keepers of the Keys, by Nicholas Cheetham
The Popes, by Eric John

"The Arabs"
Andalusian Lyrical Poetry and Old Spanish Love Songs,
     by Linda P. Compton
The Arab Mind, by Raphael Patai

"William Rufus"
William Rufus, by Frank Barlow
The Reign of William Rufus, 2 volumes, by Edward Freeman

"Edward II"
Edward II, by Harold Hutchison
The Three Edwards, by Thomas B. Costain

"Suleiman the Magnificent"
The Ottoman Empire, by Lord Kinross
Suleiman the Magnificent, by Sir Valentine Chirol

"American Indians"
The Maya World, by Demetrio S. Morales
Patterns of Culture, by Ruth Benedict

"Christopher Marlow"
Who Was Kit Marlow?, by Della Hilton
Christopher Marlow, by Gerald Pinciss

"Henri III"
Henri III: Maligned or Malignant King?, by Keith Cameron
Catherine de Medici, by Jean Heritier

"James I"
Buckingham, by Roger Lockyer
King James, by Antonia Fraser

"The Pirates"
Sodomy and the Perception of Evil, by Barry R. Burg
The Buccaneers of America, by A.O. Exquemelin

"Queen Christina"
Christina of Sweden, by Curt Weiball
Queen Christina, by Georgina Masson

"Queen Anne"
In the Day of Queen Anne, by John Rolfe
Sarah, Duchess of Marlborough, by Henry Marchon

"Frederick the Great"
Frederick the Great, edited by Louis Snyder
History of Frederick II of Prussia, edited by Thomas Carlyle and
    John Clive

"Colonial America"
The Diary of Michael Wigglesworth, edited by Edmund Morgan
Colonial New York, by John Fiske

"Marie Antionette"
Lesbian Lives, edited by Barbara Grier and Coletta Reid
Marie Antoinette, by Stefan Zweig

"Ladies of Llangollen"
The Ladies of Llangollen, by Marian Evans
Chase the Wild Goose, by Mary Gordon

"Emily Dickinson"
Surpassing the Love of Men, by Lillian Faderman
The Riddle of Emily Dickinson, by Rebecca Patterson

"Susan B. Anthony"
The Better Half, by Andrew Sinclair
Elizabeth Cady Stanton, Susan B. Anthony, edited by
    Ellen C. DuBois

"Sarah Orne Jewett"
Sarah Orne Jewett, by Richard Cary
Sarah Orne Jewett: Letters, edited by Richard Cary

"Herman Melville"
Melville, by Geoffrey Stone
Letters of Herman Melville, edited by Merrell R. Davis and
    William H. Gilman

"Walt Whitman"
Walt Whitman and the Body Beautiful, by Harold Aspiz
Some Friends of Walt Whitman, by Edward Carpenter

"Ludwig II of Bavaria"
The Dream King: Ludwig II of Bavaria, by Wilfrid Blunt and
    Hamish Hamilton
The Life of Richard Wagner, by Ernest Newman

"Peter I. Tchaikovsky"
The Diaries of Tchaikovsky, translated by Wladimir Lakond
The Triumph of Tchaikovsky: A Biography, by John Gee and Elliot
    Selby

"Victorian England"
Everyday Life in Victoria's England, by Cecil W. Smith
Sex, Society and History, by Vern L. Bullough

"Cleveland Street"
The Cleveland Street Scandal, by H. Montgomery Hyde
Love in Earnest, by J.E. Vincent

"Lord Alfred Douglas"
Oscar Wilde and Myself, by Lord Alfred Douglas
Oscar Wilde, The Aftermath, by H. Montgomery Hyde

"Andre Gide"
André Gide, by Albert J. Guerard
André Gide, by George D. Painter

"Roger Casement"
The Black Diaries, by Peter S. Gates and Maurice Girodias
Casement, The Flawed Hero, by Roger Sawyer

"Rasputin"
Black Night, White Snow, by Harrison E. Salisbury
My Father, by Maria Rasputin

"Lawrence of Arabia"
The T.E. Lawrence Puzzle, by Stephen E. Tabachnick
Seven Pillars of Wisdom, by T.E. Lawrence

"Gertrude Stein"
The Lost Generation, by Hayward H. Brune
Paris in the Twenties, by Thomas Wood

"Virginia Woolf"
Virginia Woolf: A Biography, by Quentin Bell
Virginia Woolf, by Michael Rosenthal

"Willa Cather"
Willa: The Life of Willa Cather, by Phyllis C. Robinson
Willa Cather, by Philip G. Twayne

"Ernst Roehm"
The Night of Long Knives, by Max Gallo
Sex and Society in Nazi Germany, by Hans P. Bleuel

"The Pink Triangle"
The Men with the Pink Triangle, by Heinz Heger
The Pink Triangle, by Rudiger Lautmann

"Eleanor Roosevelt"
Eleanor Roosevelt, by William T. Young
The Life of Lorena Hickok, by Doris Faber

"Joseph McCarthy"
Red Tide in America, by John Garrison
The Great Fear, by Michael Morrison

"James Dean"
Hollywood Babylon II, by Kenneth Angers
The Hollywood Reporter, by Tichi Wilkerson and Marcia Borie

"Christopher Isherwood"
Christopher Isherwood: Myth and Anti-myth, by Paul Piazza
Isherwood, by Jonathan Fryer

About the author:

Terry Boughner received his Ph.D. in history from The Catholic University of America and served as a Professor of History at La Roche College from 1969 to 1983. Since then he has been a freelance writer, and his articles on homosexuality in history have appeared in numerous gay and lesbian publications. He is currently a resident of Milwaukee, where he is the co-owner and editor of *Wisconsin Light,* the state's gay and lesbian newspaper. *Out of All Time* is his first book.

A wide variety of books with gay and lesbian
themes are available from Alyson Publications.
For a catalog, or to be placed on our mailing list,
please write to:
Alyson Publications
40 Plympton Street
Boston, Mass. 02118.